The Published Author's Guide to Promotion

◆

Marketing Tips by Published Authors

PublishAmerica

Baltimore

First printing

ISBN: 1-4137-1521-4
PUBLISHED BY PUBLISHAMERICA, LLLP
www.publishamerica.com
Baltimore

Printed in the United States of America

Table of Contents

New and Foreign Perspectives

Overall Tips and Suggestions

The Published Author's Guide to Promotion

♦

Marketing Tips by Published Authors

Introduction

by Andrea Higgins, PublishAmerica Editor

"Have you written something I would recognize?" they ask. That's when your stomach clenches and you wonder if you should have said anything at all.

"Well, no. Not YET," you answer. Because someday they will know, but for now you're just another person, another author sitting at a silent book signing table, waiting for *The New York Times* review board to come knocking.

This is writing, this is being an author—just maybe not the picture they painted for you in that English class so long ago. It's the nervousness when you put pen to paper, or fingertips to keys. It's the characters in your head that you want to tell people about—ones that you can't exactly describe with your voice, but you can converse with in your mind as their images translate onto the page. It's all about the words.

And so, maybe that's why promotion is so hard for writers, because we're best when we're creating words on a page, with just ourselves and our characters. Writing? Sure. Standing up in front of a crowded room and talking about your writing? Walking up to a bookstore counter and trying to convince a lackadaisical clerk that you're the next Stephen King? Sitting at a table by yourself and timidly calling out to indifferent customers walking through the door?

Are you kidding?

But then again, it took courage to sit down at that computer or arrange that pad of paper in your lap. It took courage to start describing those characters that had taken up residence in your head, or pen that story that deserved to be told. This book is a collection of advice about how your family of PublishAmerica authors remembered that initial courage and found it again in order to share their books with the world, outside the pages of their minds.

Sure, they've stumbled on occasion. But then again, we've all held down that delete key or scribbled across the page until the ink ran dry. Promotion is a learning process—an art that requires practice and hints from others—just like the craft of writing.

As writers, we are a community, and in these pages you will find a common attitude among your PublishAmerica brethren—"This isn't just about me, it's about us and what we are going through together." Many of your writings and e-mails contained these two words: good luck. You have the support; you need only reach out. Read this book and the tools will be at your disposal.

Don't ever forget the power of the most primitive form of promotion: word of mouth. It's quite simple: if you don't speak, nobody will hear. You must first have a strong conviction in your book. Once that foundation is built, you can pass your outlook on to everyone you meet. Don't be afraid to tell people about the newest addition to the literary world. If you don't believe, neither will they.

Napoleon Bonaparte once said, "Victory belongs to the most persevering." We must work, and work, and work for the best things in life. We all know the stories about rejection letter after rejection letter, often as first-hand accounts. Getting your book published is just the first step in the war—you've won that battle...now on to the next. When it comes to promotion, expect the same resistance that you experienced in getting your book published and you'll be one step ahead of the game.

Among other things, our published authors know the power of a press kit. While good will, optimism, and word of mouth will get you far, it's always good to make like a Boy Scout and be prepared. In a society inundated with authors, be the one who is always organized and ready to go. It's good to be an individual, but, in this case, follow the mainstream and give the bookstore exactly what it needs in order to positively assist your promotion. A fully functioning press kit, with all the necessary information, is the most efficient way to get what you want.

The Published Author's Guide to Promotion is your map, written by those who have come before you, and passed on in order for you to succeed. Find the wisdom in their words and you'll glean all the information necessary to promote your work. You wrote to share with the world—go out and do it.

Oh, and next time they ask if they would recognize your writing, say, "Yes, you will, as soon as I get finished telling you about it..."

Self-Promotion

Alternative Promoting

Lynn Barry

Running a diner and being a published author has given me the opportunity to promote my work, and work at the same time. I have a display by the diner door with a picture of me at a book signing I attended at the Barnes & Noble at Clemson University in Clemson, South Carolina, in the summer of 2002 with many other PublishAmerica authors, and a stack of books that hungry-for-more-than-food customers can not only purchase but get signed by me, the author/waitress/co-owner (it's a mom-and-pop operation).

It is a heart-pounding thrill for me when someone wants a signed copy. This type of promoting takes the stress away. When someone is interested, they approach me at the register, ask me to sign a copy, pay me and are on their way; no author sitting at a table wondering if anyone will pick the book up, let alone buy it.

At times, people have purchased the book for others; a sister who has cancer, a daughter who is going back to college as a non-trad (*Bjoyfl* is about a non-trad student), a wife.

I also have my business card available. Lots of customers have picked them up at the register.

I have had my second book available and many people who have purchased a copy now want my first book. Several readers have begun discussions about the plot of my books with other customers. What an ego booster that is for the author; little, old, coffee-serving me.

My books are also available at the library, which is located across the street from the diner. I enjoy it when an occasional customer lets me know they've checked out my books from the library. The most amusing comment so far has been the following:

"I got your book, *Puddles*, out of the library," a customer told me one day.

"Oh, you did, did you?" I responded.

"My daughter flipped through it and said she saw some bad words." She looked at me disapprovingly.

I said, "Oh, you're in for a treat!" And then I laughed.

She left, telling me she was going home to read the book.

The next day she came in and said, "I loved it!"

She also said she was going to check out my second book, *Bjoyfl* next…

"Alternative promoting," that's what I call what I do. On a daily basis, someone asks me about my books. One book at a time, I am securing a following and giving myself a tremendous amount of joy and author satisfaction. That's what it's all about, in my book!

Lynn Barry is the author of *Puddles* and *Bjoyfl*

Be Positive, Persistent, and Persevere

Elaine Bunbury

What Hope Have You! is the title of my novel, which is a story about the effects of colonialism and apartheid upon women and their families in South Africa, particularly black women and those of mixed race. This title is an exclamation and not a question because it WAS amazing that black people always expressed joy and hope in spite of their oppression. However, I phrase the words as a question when I ask myself, what hope have YOU (an unknown author; a woman past retirement age) of getting publicity and promoting my own published book? The media and bookstores are mostly interested in celebrities, either famous or infamous! As I ponder this question, I consider the subtext of my novel, which is overcoming adversity; about how black people in South Africa overcame. Inspired by Nelson Mandela, they were always hopeful; optimistic and positive; persistent and persevering; and so I apply this to my "published author's guide to promotion." That is — be positive, persistent, and persevere.

I triggered an interview with a local television station through being persistent. I first e-mailed a request, followed by telephone calls, until an interview was granted. The interview was successful and aired several times. With the local newspaper, however, I called on the book reviewer in person. At first, her response was negative and she rejected my request, citing the number of books already on her desk waiting to be reviewed. I persisted, explaining my motivation for writing this book, which I presented to her with a brief outline. She finally agreed and the review she published was positive.

Besides being persistent, one should also be alert as to what is being written about in newspapers and magazines and watch for news items on subjects that might relate to one's book. AIDS is frequently in the news, and, as this is a subject with connections to my novel, I have noted with interest the news that the American administration recognizes AIDS as not just a problem for Africa, but a world problem, and has allocated a large sum of money to fight AIDS. President Bush has been to South Africa and has visited other African countries, discussing the AIDS crisis.

In this regard, I recently read an editorial in a local magazine, "Focus On Women" about a local student doing post-graduate work on AIDS in South Africa. She writes, "Apartheid may be gone, but its legacy of an impoverished, uneducated non-white community lives on…apartheid, men going off to work in the mines…have led to the breakdown of non-white families and society." As this is what I am attempting to show in my book — that apartheid caused the breakdown of black family life, contributing to the spread of AIDS — I took the opportunity to e-mail a letter to the editor. I had no response. I had contacted this magazine previously, but with no interest shown. I refused to be discouraged and sent the letter again. This time I did receive a positive reply. The editor requested a copy of my book, as she realized it related to the subject of her editorial. She informed me she would publish my letter in the an edition of the magazine, and has promised to pass my book on to be reviewed. Persistence and being alert prevailed!

Bookstores are sometimes more difficult to approach. Many are hesitant about ordering books by unknown authors. Another problem has been the high exchange rate and sales tax levied in Canada, causing bookstore owners to consider the book too highly priced for a paperback. This was brought to the attention of PublishAmerica, who now offers a bigger discount to Canadian booksellers. I approached the librarian at the public library about a book signing and reading, and, once again, persisted until a date was set. We advertised it well, and I was told it was the best-attended reading they had ever had. The library also bought copies of the book.

I control my nervousness before and during public speaking by believing in the message of my book. I WANT to tell this story. I WANT it known how black workers, such as those on the mines and in government employ, were prohibited by law from having their spouses living with them. They were housed in compounds, only able to visit their wives once a year. In the case of domestic servants, they were accommodated in backyard rooms in the suburbs in single quarters. Prostitution was rife and this contributed to the spread of AIDS. I believe that if the public understands that many of South Africa's present problems are a direct result of past policies of apartheid, this understanding will encourage not only contributions to funding for medication to finding a cure for AIDS, but will also help establishing an infrastructure for clinics to operate to educate the people who are misled by many false myths such as, "having sex with a virgin will cure a man of AIDS." (This was a belief held by men in England in the 19th century for curing syphilis!)

Foreign investment is also needed in South Africa to create jobs, enabling people to work and help themselves. Many novels today are about dysfunctional families; *What Hope Have You!* is about a dysfunctional country. Although apartheid is over, we must not forget its affects because, "those who do not remember the past are condemned to repeat it" (George Santayana). This strong conviction and desire that people understand why South Africa still has problems, after apartheid has ended, enables me to overcome my nervousness when speaking in public.

DO maintain a positive attitude, be persistent and persevere in spite of negative responses. DON'T be discouraged by rejection nor detracted from promoting your work.

Handouts do help. I have cards, advertising my book, my website and bookstores where it is available, as well as other relevant information which I keep with me and hand out when appropriate. Making use of the Internet and having a website also contributes to promoting your work.

I am becoming known in the local community. I live in a small town, but I am now promoting my book in a neighboring, much-larger city where I have a book signing and reading in their public library arranged. Their local daily newspaper, which I approached repeatedly, has now requested a copy of my book for review purposes.

In conclusion, my published author's guide to promotion is be positive, persistent, and persevere.

Elaine Bunbury is the author of *What Hope Have You!*

A Few of the Things I Did to Promote My Fantasy Novel

Diana Hignutt

I had a lot of naive ideas in my head about the publishing business when I was offered my first contract. I had written a fantasy novel, and fantasy was hot. I thought I had it made. As I quickly discovered, unless you are a formerly unemployed British lady who writes books about a punk kid wizard, it's not that easy to get people interested in giving you publicity. As a direct result of my first rejections at the hands of bookstore managers and newspaper editors, I realized that I either had to give up, or put up with the occasional kick in the teeth, and try to find more creative ways to get people interested in me and my book. The most important advice I can offer you is to never give up, no matter how tough things seem; no matter how many roadblocks you face, keep trying. An author I admire told me recently that I was sure to be a success because of my perpetual optimism and positive thinking. Develop those traits, and you can not fail, because you will never stop trying.

Now, let's get down to the hard tacks of my promotional efforts. The very first thing I did, even before my book came out, was to have bookmarks, flyers and a giant poster of my book made (I used the cover art and had pros do the work). You will need a good supply of these things for signings, conventions, etc. And a giant poster of your book cover, tastefully displayed on an easel, really does set you apart as a pro at your events.

I built a website, which I constantly update and maintain. There I list my professional reviews, events, news, book ordering information, etc. Now, I must confess to being a recently reformed computer Luddite, but it was easy and fun. There are lots of companies that offer free web hosting (with websites that practically build themselves) or do so at a very low cost. To get some ideas, check out my website at *www.authorsden.com/dianahignutt*. If I can do it, you can do it. With these preparations made, I was ready.

When my fantasy novel, *Moonsword*, first came out I bought a medieval princess costume, put it on, drove to downtown Philadelphia, and passed out my flyers on a busy corner (just across the street from both Barnes & Noble and Borders). Sure, I got funny looks, but a few hundred people learned about my book that day.

I sent out lots of press kits to every local and regional paper, some metropolitan papers, and genre magazines. I made sure to emphasize my real-life connection to my story. In my case, my novel is a faerie-tale thriller about a prince who is transformed into a woman, and I happen to be a post-op transsexual woman. I played that up. (My original press release is posted on my website, if you're interested). A couple of papers did stories on me, most didn't. I just couldn't attract the attention of the book editor at the major Philadelphia newspaper I wanted. So, I found the people columnist, and sent my stuff to him. I pestered him just enough. He wrote a great story on my personal transformation and my (and my wife's) legal same-sex marriage, and because my life situation tied in so well with my book, a lot of people picked up on my story and a fair number of folks bought my book. I got three calls to do radio interviews and one national TV interview (*The O'Reilly Factor*). From my successful appearance on *The O'Reilly Factor*, I got another interview on the same network.

Now, the national TV appearances opened a lot of doors for me. Bookstores that had refused to talk to me before wanted me for book signings, etc. Radio stations from all over the country called. The trick is to build on your success. Parlay the small breaks into bigger ones. With my name "out there," I was able to get a short story accepted by a national magazine and was asked to contribute another story for an upcoming anthology project. These should help build a fan base and get people interested in my book. I'm now targeting more national TV talk shows.

Another trick is to network. Network with other writers and find ways to help each other: review swapping, marketing idea exchange, etc. I used Amazon.com as a tool for this. The page for my book there lists other books purchased by people who bought my book. I did a little research and contacted the authors of those books. Most were very happy to hear from me. From these contacts, I learned a lot about the publishing business (much that was specific to my genre), I got some great reviews, and new marketing ideas, and I was asked to participate in that anthology project I mentioned. I also made some terrific literary friends.

So, those are some of my ideas. Use whatever you have at your disposal. If there is something interesting about you and it ties in at all with your book, use it as a promotional tool. Okay, you're probably not a transsexual, but I bet if you think about it, there is something special and unique about you or your life that ties in with your book. Use it. Also, make sure you follow up every bit of promotion you do. If you get rejected (and you will, be ready for that), find out what the bookstore manager, newspaper editor, or producer didn't like about your pitch, and use that information to hone your next attempt. Be smart, be confident, be assertive, be persistent, be polite, don't give up, and get busy promoting yourself and your book.

Diana Hignutt is the author of *Moonsword*

Visibility!

Naomi Johnson

Visibility!...Visibility!...Visibility!....and yet again, Visibility!

No matter what line of work you are involved in, it is important that you make yourself as visible as possible. Keeping the public aware of your presence is now, and has always been, the focal point of getting sales and invitations. It is the reason that McDonald's has the "Golden Arches," that Kentucky Fried Chicken has the "Colonel," that Blue Belle (if you're from the South) has the cow "Blue Belle." You get the point — make yourself as visible as you can possibly make yourself, and watch what happens!

Get out of the box! Most people miss opportunities to market themselves and their products because they look for the obvious. Look for the not so obvious and the not so routine to get your ideas, your persona, and your product into the public eye. Is there a community event this weekend that is an outdoor/indoor event? Great, get your "handouts" put onto colorful paper, call a few friends, and get out to the weekend event. Pass out the flyers as you mill around and don't let the grass grow under your feet; talk to people about what you are doing and your product. Let them know whom you are and what you have to share. Invite them to your next reading or signing.

Get involved! Find a community group or two and roll up your sleeves. Youth groups, book clubs, and actors' guilds are always looking for people who write, sing, dance, or can simply paint a wall. It is a great way to meet new people and to have your new group sponsor your next reading or signing or reception. People love to help their own, just be sincere in your signing on with the group to meet their needs, and you will find the doors open to meet your needs as well.

When you work with little theater groups, the media is almost always around. Make yourself friendly, share a little of whom you are, why you are there and watch for indication of who is interested. Go to your local newspapers and ask for interviews about your upcoming events and literary works. Invite the media to a reading or signing or reception. Volunteer to do an article for the local newspaper; they are often looking for just the right someone they can use to fill some void — fill the void yourself!

Getting into local bookstores is sometimes difficult. Find two or three that cater to the type of literature that you have to offer. Approach the owners/ managers about putting your books on their shelves, and in return offer to sign books in the store as a precursor to letting the public know that you're housed in their shop. While there are three bookstores in my town, I am exclusive with only one; this was a great sales pitch for the owner because she wanted to set up "something special" in her shop in which customers could come for an afternoon, once a month, to meet a particular author. She is billed as an exclusive shop, which is a prestigious undertaking and to be a part of the shop is distinctive. Don't forget to contact bookstores in surrounding cities about becoming a part of their "reading/signing" programs.

Set up receptions and programs in your hometown and surrounding areas to promote your new literary releases. Invite local talent and celebrities to appear on the program with you. Build your program around your newest literary piece and let those who know you help to promote you, as you have done for them. Make sure that you have lots of entertainment and food. Don't forget to have lots of your books on hand to sign and sell; after all, that is the reason you are having the reception in the first place.

Don't forget to contact local clubs, dinner clubs, fraternities, or sororities. Make yourself available to them for speaking engagements. They are always looking for speakers, and who is of more interest than local authors and celebrities? Take your books and order forms along on these excursions and your invitations and sales will continue to increase. You should expect to get at least two invitations from each of these speaking engagements, or more!

Start an authors' group, let the city know that you are a part of the authors' group or guild and that you do special activities together, or individually, to benefit local groups. We raised scholarship monies for underprivileged children last year by having community productions in which authors were on the programs to perform or just be present to meet the audience. It keeps you in the limelight and supports your fellow authors while promoting everyone's work. In essence, you are visible!

Naomi Johnson is the author of *Lights on in the Window*

How Did I Go Where No Author Had Gone Before?

Christopher Bonn Jonnes

Looking to branch out from traditional bookstore sales outlets, I sent the following PR release to my local Harley-Davidson Motorcycle dealership (I'm an avid rider and a regular customer).

St. Croix Harley-Davidson Customer Publishes Novel

Okay, so I'm not Peter Fonda or Jay Leno, but you can add another celebrity to the swelling ranks of Harleywood. I'm a regular in New Richmond, and I used the serenity of long solo rides to and from the SCHD dealership to flesh out the story in my new suspense novel, which earned a book publishing contract in a national fiction contest. My book, *Wake Up Dead*, was released April 15 in paperback. The sales are huge, and the book is getting solid 5-star reviews on both Barnes&Noble.com and Amazon.com. Amazon claims my book is the #1 bestseller in Stillwater, MN. That's better than the governor's *I Ain't Got Time To Bleed*. I'm kicking Jesse Ventura's ass, and there ain't nothin' he can do about it. Book information is available on my website at *http://www.BonnJonnes.com*.

They loved the memo so much, they ran it verbatim in their newsletter, invited me to do two book signings at the dealership, and purchased a huge pile of books, which they placed prominently on their counter. They sold every one. They were more receptive and supportive than my local bookstore.

The following is the text of my sales message that went via mail, e-mail, hand, and any means possible to potential buyers. It became the single most successful tool I had, generating many book sales and laughs. The letter is still listed on my website.

Reasons to Buy *Wake Up Dead*:

I wrote a book. It's good. It's not very wordy. It got published. It's for sale. My publisher asked me to "market" it. I said okay. Please buy a copy. The book is a suspense novel in paperback and numerous eBook formats, and is now in its second printing. It has great crossover appeal to mystery and sci-fi lovers. Not sold yet? Here are reasons to buy the book.

It's good
It's cheap
It's lightweight
It's compact
It's durable
It's disposable
It's my last if it doesn't sell

And best of all, imagine the benefits of being a close, personal friend of a truly rich and famous person. You can live vicariously through me as I cruise the streets of Hollywood in an expensive sports car and cavort with beautiful people.

The book also makes a great gift idea. Remember, it's never too early to start Christmas shopping. Give a copy to your favorite friends and relatives. Get an autographed copy and brag about the people you rub elbows with. Autographed copies are available directly from me: *http:// www.bonnjonnes.com/autogrph.html*.

Books are also available from your favorite store. If not in stock, they'll need the author's name, book title, and ISBN number (0-9664520-5-4) to special order it for you. Or buy it from many other booksellers: *http:// www.bonnjonnes.com/order.html*.

PARTIAL LIST OF USES:
Read it.
Display it and tell people, "Oh yeah, I'm a good friend of the author."
Hold it in up public places and look "intellectual."

Do #2 or #3 in a bar for free drinks or sex.
Keep it by the fireplace for kindling.
Store a copy at the cabin for emergency toilet paper.
Line the bottom of the birdcage.
199 pages equals 199 paper airplanes.
Use the pages for target practice at the range.
Exercise your shredder.
Sell your "signed original" at the garage sale and make a profit.
Origami
Papier mâche
Chew toy for Fido.
Shim that wobbly furniture.
Populate the bookshelf.
Read it to a group at the nursing home when serving your "community service."
Throw it off the doomed Stillwater Lift Bridge as a farewell token.
Show it to the police when pulled over and say, "Do you know who I am?"
Tear out the pages and try to buy your groceries with them.
Door jam.
Make pressed flowers.
Cut a hole in the middle and hide things inside.
Use the crumpled pages as packing material.
Throw it at the cat for licking the butter.

Everyone should buy at least six autographed copies: *http://www.bonnjonnes.com/autogrph.html*.

Here's what 218 readers have to say about *Wake Up Dead*: *http://www.bonnjonnes.com/reviews.html*.

UPDATE: We sold the movie rights for *Wake Up Dead*! *http://www.bonnjonnes.com/rights.html*

My second suspense novel, *Big Ice*, *http://www.bonnjonnes.com/bigice.html*, is now available for sale.

Thank you for your support!
Christopher Bonn Jonnes
Famous Author & Regular Guy

Christopher Bonn Jonnes is the author of *Big Ice* and *Wake Up Dead*

How Did I Become a Local Celebrity?

Laura Klotz

There's one piece of advice that I feel very compelled to share, and that's this: People will be more excited about what you have to offer if you make them understand how it will benefit them. I was very fortunate in that, around the time my book was being released, a small newspaper was opening up in my very tiny hometown. I immediately contacted the editor about printing my press release, and he was very enthusiastic. Because their first issue mentioned a need for writers, I came up with a way to tie in their needs with mine. My book focuses on the difference that committed volunteers can make, so I suggested to the editor that I start writing a regular column for him which spotlighted local volunteer efforts and projects. He immediately took me up on the offer, and my first column ran two weeks later. The pay isn't very high, but I don't mind because the column accomplishes many goals all at once — it generates publicity for my writing, it gives my editor a regular, well-written feature, and it increases interest in local charities and volunteer organizations, many of which would go virtually unknown otherwise. Everybody benefits! It also came in handy a little later, when the town organized its anniversary festival and invited me to come and do a book signing at one of the booths; people who knew me from my column came to find out more about my book. If you can find a way for your book's subject to fill a need in your community, it will virtually sell itself.

Laura Klotz is the author of *Saving the World in Your Spare Time:*
The Pocket Guide to Effecting Positive Change

Suggestions for New Authors
Patricia Nelson

It is good to *keep your name in the public eye* after the initial flurry of media exposure. When an opportunity arises to appear in public, grab it!

Calls may come in from service organizations asking you to be a guest speaker. So what if you are nervous about talking to groups? Do it anyway. Audiences are generally friendly and supportive, and anxious to hear your experience. Writing is your forte, not theirs, so you have one leg up on them. Bring along copies of your book should anyone wish to buy that day, and give clear information on where else they can be purchased (online or in stores).

Better yet, be proactive and contact the civic groups, senior citizens' centers, Scout troops, schools, etc. yourself (as appropriate for your type of book) and offer to be a guest speaker. Notify the Chamber of Commerce that you are available should they get requests from their members. Your topic could be the life of a writer, or discussing the book's content (especially if it is non-fiction).

If you have the time and inclination, expand the areas in which you write. Be the newsletter editor for an organization. Submit articles to magazines of all sizes (it's tough to get work accepted there as well, but you just might luck out). Ask to write a feature for the local newspaper if a story catches your eye. All of these endeavors remind people that you are a writer, plus they look good on query letters as you summarize your experience and publishing history. You are setting up a network that will likely pay off down the road.

In my case, I volunteered to write and direct a Christmas play for use at our church. The performance went over so well, I wrote another for the following year, and will probably get to do this as long as I wish. I also contacted the city library about their summer activity schedule for children. I wrote a play and conducted a drama camp for youngsters. We presented the play to the public the last day. For this activity, there was a participation fee (my stipend). Local newspaper coverage of the event brought me free publicity. A number of people hope I will keep this program going. A woman in the audience asked if I could possibly write a play for the members of the senior center where she works (and where I had spoken previously). I will also charge for that. I keep the copyright to all these plays, and someday they may be published.

So, one thing leads to another, and behind it all, people know I am an author. They often ask when another book will be coming out. Besides keeping the creative juices flowing, writing introduces me to so many wonderful people who respect what I do. The same will be true for you.

Patricia Nelson is the author of *Cool Spring*

World Wide Web

◆

Online Friends

Frank Allen

I became an active member of an online writers' forum nearly two years ago, and, as a result, I have made literally hundreds of friends nationwide as well as from all over the world. I'm certain that I've now sold my book even outside of the continental U.S. to some readers in Puerto Rico, Great Britain, Australia, New Zealand and the United Arab Emirates.

When I say "online friends," please don't mistake that to mean that they are merely faceless characters at some site. Quite the contrary is the case. We exchange cards, letters and gifts through traditional mail and talk on the telephone on a regular basis. Yes, we're actual friends. You must remember that there are real people behind every computer screen.

I have a huge fan base there at that site and some of them have even sent me their copy of my book so that I could sign it and send it back to them. Of course, I was more than happy to do so. It's a unique feeling to be asked for an autograph. It makes you feel appreciated and lets you know that you've done something that was worthwhile to someone. You can't put a price on that.

I also set up my own website and promoted my book there. I put various facets of my personality into that site and I mentioned the book often throughout its almost-thirty pages. A friend of mine in England also placed it prominently on another site and, thanks to her, it's now listed in most, if not all, search engines.

To all aspiring authors, I wish you well in your endeavors. My hope is that you have the same success that I've enjoyed. Get out there, be it online or otherwise. Just be yourself, make some friends and let everyone you meet know about your work. Do that and you'll surely be rewarded in more ways than one.

Frank Allen is the author of *Bedtime Tales Your Parents Never Told You*

Promoting Yourself by E-mail
Betty S. Almond

Authors often believe that once their book is published, the work is finished. Not true. Like any product, a book is successful only if it reaches an audience.

Consider the number of times you see name-brand commercials. Most of those products are household words because the pitch is "out there." The business has been established. Money has been made. The product has proven sales. Yet, the commercials continue. Why? The answer is simple: Repetition brings remembrance.

You can send out your own commercials using a periodical online mailing with announcements of new and upcoming releases. In order to utilize this type of "commercial," you must build a professional e-mail list. How do you set up and build a list? Start with friends and associates.

First, open your online server address book. Set up a new group titled "Promo List." Within this group, list all the screen names of friends and associates you've met online. Be sure to use the BCC (blind carbon copy) function for this list; otherwise, anyone receiving your promotional mailing will be displeased to discover that their name (and everyone else's) is visible to others on the list. Common courtesy dictates that you do not divulge another's screen name.

Another source of adding e-mail names to your list is to provide a guest book on your professional website and include the screen names of those that have signed it. Also, on the cover page of your website, be sure to include an option with a direct-mail-to-you link that reads:

To be placed on my professional updates mail list, click here and type add in the subject line. Thanks!

Finally, you can gather screen names during any chats you visit by asking politely whether anyone in the room would like to be placed on your professional mailing list. This method is best used in casual chat rooms rather than during a scheduled chat. However, most chat hosts will not frown if you make a short comment into the chat room before a chat begins or after it ends such as, "I've got a new book out! E-mail or IM me if you'd like to get my professional updates via e-mail and I'll add you to the list." A note of warning: Never make a pest of yourself by imposing upon a protocol chat or one that is not open to comments about other's news. This kind of intrusion can bring serious repercussions in the form of being tossed or losing your online service. Avoid spam!

Once you have a mail list, keep in mind as you prepare your mail-out to include a statement for the recipient's request of removal from the list. This statement is essential in order to protect your online status. Being reported to your online service for spamming is a serious matter. You might consider using the following statement:

Have a great day and, as always, if you wish to be removed from my personal updates list, hit reply and type remove in the body of the e-mail.

Never assume associates and friends or slight acquaintances will welcome your updates. Because you want to promote good will along with your work, always remove any name from the list if someone requests removal. Even if you are crushed by a friend's request of removal from your list, DO NOT respond with any comments other than to say "Thank you."

In the body of your mailing, announce all upcoming speaking engagements, book releases and book purchase information, as well as any other events you have scheduled within the mailing time frame. If you are planning to be a guest speaker in an online chat, provide a link to the chat room, and the date and time of the chat. Don't forget to provide listings of links to various online sites that feature your work. Also, you should include a link to your professional website that has samples of your work and a professional resume.

Using your mail list, you can also establish a monthly newsletter that features the latest announcements and even those of your associates. Another way to promote your work and build your audience is to include a short story, poem, article or an excerpt from your latest book. After all, product manufacturers give free samples and coupons. If it works for them, it will work for you.

Whether you develop a newsletter or a single e-mail promotional update, consider including helpful links to online areas that have helped you as a writer. Research links, a favorite market site, or a brief mention of the name and area where you've taken beneficial online classes are a few links that others would appreciate. You may even offer those receiving the newsletter an opportunity to include some of their announcements in your next mailing as a thank you and acknowledgment that you are willing to help them while helping promote your own work.

Whatever you decide to include in your mailing, remember that if you can interest one individual, you've gained a prospective book buyer.

Betty Almond (DeLoris Spires) isthe author of *Like a Promise*, *Almond Eyes*, and *Harm's Done*

Success Through Association
Danielle M. Angeline

Fortunately, the release of my book came right around the time of my 20-year, high school reunion. Because I grew up in a community where everybody knew everybody, I easily enlisted the help of my high school reunion coordinator. Since the advent of the Internet, reunion committees are finding it easier to build e-mail address data banks; therefore, the reunion coordinator was happy to send out a mass e-mail announcement to my fellow classmates from high school. It reached some 400+ graduates and word has spread to their older and younger siblings.

I now have a posting about my book on my high school's website that covers all sorts of information for all graduating classes as far back as the early 1960s. Because of one simple e-mail announcement, it also reached a book reviewer at the local paper where I grew up and they contacted me for an interview. Ironically, the mass e-mail, the post on the website and the interview cost me nothing except maybe a little driving time, and it was well worth it.

I encourage new authors to contact any and all schools they may be associated with, including their college(s). Colleges and universities use success stories to their advantage to lure new students, and who wouldn't want to attend a college that has turned out a published author?

All in all, approach any organization you may be affiliated with: high school, college, volunteer group, business group, church, clubs, etc. I found that most associations charge nominal fees for advertising/announcements of a book release. What I found works best is to offer them a free autographed copy of your book — it opened a lot of doors for me.

Danielle M. Angeline is the author of *The Sterling Series*: *Personally or Professionally, Lost and Found* (December 2003), *Always and Forever* (June 2004)

The
"Three Musketeers Approach"
Ivan and Dora Cain

As for promoting our book *The Year 2012*, we found it most helpful to gather many authors together on websites, that we designed, to list the author's name and title, plus a picture of the book cover, a brief paragraph about the book, and another about the author. We then link the book cover to their personal website, plus we link their title to the two major online book stores, Amazon.com and Barnes & Noble. We call this the "Three Musketeers approach." (All for one, and one for all.)

As each author that is posted on the websites tell others where they can find their book, they automatically help promote all the other authors on the sites. All of our websites are listed on search engines, plus we use all the free ads available on the Internet. Listed below are the websites. Please check them out. You will get a better picture of what we have noted. These provide free posting for authors.

http://www.ivandoracain.faithweb.com
http://year2012.freeservers.com
http://www.authorshowcase2.freeservers.com

We also are setting up another website just for authors that write about the end-time prophecy: *http://watchman.faithweb.com*

Ivan and Dora Cain are the authors of *The Year 2012*

Marketing on the Cheap
Thomas Farrell

The Internet presents a vast opportunity for creative marketing. I have used four techniques to drive sales, none of which have cost me a penny.

1. Develop a website. This can be done easily, and for free, by using tools available from Yahoo's Geocities, for example. If you go that route, it will be necessary to acquire a Yahoo e-mail address, and I recommend creating one that is uniquely tied in to your book. For example, my e-mail address for author correspondence is thejessicaproject@yahoo.com

Once you have set up a special-purpose e-mail address, you can follow the idiot-proof steps at Geocities to perfect your website, which can include a picture of your book cover as well as links to PublishAmerica, Amazon, and Barnes & Noble so visitors can buy your book with a mouse click or two. Of course, you can spend some money and get a more elaborate website with your own domain name, but a free website will be perfectly suitable for marketing your book. My web address is *www.geocities.com/thejessicaproject/author*

Remember to include your website on all your promotional material, correspondence, and other collateral.

2. Now that you have a website, you can surf the net, looking for like-minded individuals who might be interested in the subject matter of your book. Let's suppose you wrote a book about hunting. Enter hunting in the major search engines, and find websites devoted to the subject. Look for the ones that feature message boards, and check out the ones that have the most activity. You can join these message boards, and look for an opportunity to pitch your book. CAUTION: There is a fine line between information and spam. If you go overboard, you will turn off everybody in the group, and maybe even get banned from it. Take it from me, I learned this the hard way.

Yahoo has hundreds of groups for members who share a common interest, and they can be approached the same way. Some of these websites and groups will lead you to the e-mail addresses of the members, which will let you put the third technique to work.

3. Create a clever promotion for your book, imbedding a picture of your book cover and a link to your website. Some of the message boards referred to above, such as Flowgo, will allow you to create messages with images and links, and you can cut and paste the finished product right into an e-mail message, which you can then send out to prospective readers. For example, I poked fun at Al Gore's foundering book sales with this little gem:

SLEEPER NOVEL SWAMPS GORE

In another humiliating setback for the former Vice President, his new book, *Joined at the Heart*, has fallen behind *The Jessica Project*, Thomas Farrell's romantic thriller, on the Amazon sales charts. Industry analysts were stunned by this development, particularly in light of the promotional fanfare which accompanied Gore's literary effort when it was published late last year. By contrast, *The Jessica Project*, released with limited marketing and bookstore distribution, has climbed steadily on the Amazon charts. Last week, *The Jessica Project*, which features an oddball romance between a cross-dressing assassin and a beautiful federal agent, ranked in the top 1% of over 1500 titles currently available from PublishAmerica on Amazon. Farrell was at a loss to explain the success of his first novel. Gore was not available for comment.

Click here [provide link to your book] to find The Jessica Project at Amazon.com

4. Finally, consider posting some of your other writing on the web, as a way of showing potential readers what you're capable of producing. If your novel is a romance, search the web for sites featuring short stories in that genre, then sit down and write a short story that will knock their socks off. When you post it, always include a tag line referring to your book (I use "by the author of The Jessica Project") and look for sites that allow you to include a link to your website. Some of my stories have had over 10,000 "hits" apiece on multiple websites, and I know they have resulted in book sales because I

have gotten e-mails from readers who told me so. Here is an example (note that I have used a nom de plume as my Internet screen name):

http://www2.storysite.org/story/questionsformissbutl~01.html

So there you have it, four easy ways to market on the cheap by using the power of the Internet. None of the above techniques is any more crass than the shameless book promotions engaged in by celebrities every day; they can be a lot of fun, and best of all, they're free.

Thomas Farrell is the author of *The Jessica Project*

Becoming the "Resident Author"
Sherry L. Gibson

Join a lot of online groups as soon as your book is accepted for publication. By joining online groups, you extend your circle of online friends. Be active in the group discussions. I suggest they not all be reading and writing groups, though those are good choices. Many other aspiring authors will be in those groups and you may feel in competition for interest in your book.

The variety of online groups is varied and wide. If you have a health problem, find support groups with similar problems. Make friends! I have found that friends I've made through numerous online health-support groups have been very encouraging to me and have purchased a lot of my books.

Do you have pets, children, hobbies, and special interests of any kind? There is a group out there just for you. The more you expand your circle of friends and acquaintances, the better your chance of selling your book.

I belong to over 40 support groups, so I know how this works. I receive all the group posts through e-mail, which is a lot of work. I join and talk to the members about things they are interested in. It's okay to be a bit of the actor/actress here if you are having problems finding the right groups. The key is to use your imagination. Join groups to learn more about what they know, ask questions, become part of the group.

I would advise against using a hard-sale tactic. Use a soft, gentle approach. Try to remember you aren't just there to sell a book or two, but to make friends. When you are comfortable in your group and feel you are accepted as part of the group, tell them a little about yourself and your book. Gently introduce them to your book! I use many different approaches and they all work for me.

Most groups ask you for an introduction. In my introduction, I always tell them I am an author. I sometimes give them a URL to my websites. I drop little hints here and there, subtle, always subtle. I try to wait until someone asks me about my career as an author. If someone in the groups asks me the question, then I discuss it with them. I tell them about my book. I always tell them that if they are interested in knowing more about my book, they can visit my website and read the synopsis and first chapter of my book.

People have to find an approach that is comfortable for them. I might stay away from the groups for two or three days and then post an apology for being missing in action, and then follow up with an explanation of something connected to my book. I might have been too busy with book promotions to have time at the computer. It could have been time I was editing the final proof copies, or whatever. Again, use your creative imagination to catch the ear of your new friends.

When my novel, *Only a Game*, was released, I sold 20 copies almost immediately to online friends I'd met through my groups. I sold them autographed copies and mailed them out as soon as I received payment. That was not a large number of sales, considering the hours I put into setting this up. However, my goal was achieved. I had one or two from many different groups buying my book. They would read my book and then post a message to me about my book! The message would come to me, but also go to each member of the group who received all posts by e-mail. I was no longer promoting my book; my readers were doing the work for me.

You have to catch the attention of someone within each group. Hard sales are often not permitted and looked down upon. I have seen new authors banned from reading groups for the hard-sale approach. People gather together for a common bond. Your job is to make yourself part of that bond and then gently introduce your talent as an author. Once that is done and you get a few sales, then those people will do the bragging and talking for you. They will spark the interest of other readers within the group. You are slowly building the snowball affect.

People love to feel that they know an author personally. They enjoy knowing their friend is a published author. When someone new joins the group, they often introduce me as their "resident author" and I immediately have the interest of a new person.

I have also discovered how excited my long list of friends gets when I'm excited. If someone contacts me wanting to buy an autographed copy of *Only a Game*, I share my excitement with my friends. This is so easy when doing group posts by e-mail. I type one e-mail and then blind copy it to every group I belong to. This is a quick and easy way to add a subliminal message to many people all at one time. Remember, you are looking for ways, subtle or outright, to put your book in front of a vast number of people. Statistics tell me that an idea has to be presented at least four times for the average person to begin to take notice. Working with online groups, it is possible to continually put your book in front of them and still not be overwhelming to them.

While promoting my book, I also make sure that I always include PublishAmerica, so my new friends become familiar with the name. I want them to recognize the name when they are looking for books. "Authors helping other authors" is a wonderful motto for our group of writers at PublishAmerica. When I see a new book being released by PublishAmerica, I immediately share the book title and the author's name with my reading group.

Sherry L Gibson is the author of *Only a Game*

A Technique for
Specialized Books
Nina Murphy

For my first book, *SPONSORS: How to Get One; How to Keep One*, for race car drivers, I went online and went to every racing-based site I could find. When the site said "Contact us," I would e-mail them using "Sponsorship" in the subject line and then offering free space on my website (Murfink.com) in the "Rising Stars" section. No racer would overlook the magic word "Sponsorship" and I sold the rest of my supply very quickly. I recommend this technique for specialized books — children's, how-to books or other similar genres.

Nina Murphy is the author of *Dispatches From a Born-Again Cynic*

A Beneficial Website

David Lester Snell

With millions of people connected to the Internet, having a website is important, especially to a published author, because it's an effective way to advertise and showcase work. But the site must provide a crucial service, or no one will visit it. It must also be well advertised.

When PublishAmerica accepted my dark fantasy novella, *Hourglass*, I immediately launched *exit66.net*. The prototype was bare bones: Minimal graphics and loads of content. When I decided to upgrade it, I used Photoshop to create graphical links and decorations, but still kept my informational base. This way, the site attracted both those seeking facts *and* those seeking pretty pictures. Nevertheless, something was missing.

For a long time, I'd wanted to launch my own horror magazine but lacked the necessary funds. With a website, however, I could start a non-profit e-zine, which would cost nothing. Therefore, I unleashed *Hugo Horror*, adding it to the pages of *exit66*. This way, I would attract more traffic, plus provide novice writers with publication. After that, it was just a matter of making my site well known.

First, I placed a dozen adds in free classifieds all over the web, using *Hugo Horror* as my main attraction, inviting submissions. I registered with genre-specific search engines and directories like Crypt Crawl, Horrorfind, and Published.com. Then, I joined the Horror Webring and banner exchange. For every two banners I displayed on *exit66*, one of *my* banners appeared somewhere else. I was able to keep track of the resultant daily and monthly hits, which grew exponentially, probably because of *Hugo Horror*; people wanted to submit. To top it off, I swapped links with other e-zines, like *The Dream People*, still using the *Hugo Horror* focus.

So, by offering publication and by scratching backs, I was able to double my exposure. It proves that an unselfish approach is critical, even appealing. That's why, in the future, I plan to showcase other authors' books —

providing reviews, synopses, and sample chapters—because, in the end, I want *exit66* to benefit everyone involved.

David Lester Snell is the author of *Hourglass*

Three-Pronged Approach
Jay Squires

What follows is a three-pronged approach to marketing your novel. It requires the acquisition of e-mail addresses from a substantial number of "prospects."

FIRST PRONG: Send an electronic postcard (available through PublishAmerica free of charge). Choose to be notified when it is picked up.

SECOND PRONG: After it has been picked up, "paste" the following message and e-mail to the prospect:

> It dawned on me after I sent you the postcard that, rather than you ordering a copy of the book from the publisher, which you would get at the pre-release discount price of [PRICE OF YOUR BOOK], you may call me to reserve a copy, at the same price, and thereby save $3.00 shipping and handling. Once I have enough orders, I'll order them in bulk and call you when they arrive.
>
> Let me know when you order whether you'll want your copy (blush!) autographed. That way, I can personalize a message for you.
>
> At any rate, when the publisher discontinues the pre-release discount price, I shall have to, also. So please call right away if you want to reserve a copy.
>
> Thank you for your support.
>
> [YOUR NAME]
> [HOME PHONE]
> [WORK PHONE]

THIRD PRONG: After about a week has passed and you haven't been contacted for a reserved copy, e-mail the following "pasted" item:

Dear [PROSPECT'S NAME]:

When I go to Borders or Barnes & Noble to browse around and perhaps to buy a book, I let my eyes scan across the shelf of books until who-knows-what mysterious force causes first one book and then another to almost "jump out to me." Usually, it's because the cover rivets my eyes to it. I pick up the book, turn it around in my hands, and get the heft and feel of it.

Then, if it gets my attention, I examine it a little more closely. I read the synopsis on the back cover to see if I have an interest in the subject matter.

If that "test" is passed, I usually take the book to the refreshment area, buy a cup of Starbucks, sit down and open it up. "Okay, Mr. Author," I say to myself, "you've got ten pages." I know that if the author can't get me hooked in the first ten pages, he's not going to get me hooked at all. And back on the shelf it goes.

The reason I'm sending you this is because I am confident I can hook your interest in the first ten pages. I'll get to the challenge in just a moment. But, first, let me share with you what reviewers are saying about [TITLE OF YOUR BOOK].

[HERE YOU SHOULD INCLUDE TWO OR THREE OF THE BEST REVIEWS FOR YOUR NOVEL]

I want, so much, to have you enjoy [TITLE OF YOUR BOOK] that I would like to offer you the ten-page challenge right away. Just click on the attachment below. Then, kick back with your coffee or other beverage and enjoy the first chapter of [TITLE OF YOUR BOOK]. If, after that first chapter, you are hooked, call me at the number below so I can reserve an autographed copy for you.

Good Reading....

[YOUR NAME]
[FIRST TELEPHONE NUMBER] or

[SECOND TELEPHONE NUMBER] or
[E-MAIL ADDRESS]

[YOUR CHAPTER ONE ATTACHMENT]

I hope this simple, non-confrontational approach works for you. Start right now collecting those e-mail addresses!

Jay Squires is the author of *The Dead Of Winter*

Capitalize on Your Book's Areas of Interest
Stephen Yulish

I have done everything possible to help get my novel, *The Great Harpazo Deception: The Real Story of UFOs*, on as many websites as possible. That is no guarantee of success, but it can't hurt. Since my novel deals with the concept of UFOs, I managed to get it on: *www.sffworld.com*, *www.lampholder.com*, *www.thehickmanreport.com*, *www.ufoinfo.com*, *http://ufos.about.com*, and was just asked by the publisher of *UFO Digest* to send a review copy.

Since my novel also deals with the end-time Bible prophecy, I have managed to get it on:

www.jewishvoice.com
www.prophezine.com
www.ohlook.ohzone.net
www.heartofisrael.org
www.armaggedonbooks.com
www.mayimhayim.org
www.raptureready.com
www.messianic-literary.com.

Since my book is fiction, I also did an interview with *www.fictionforum.net* and my novel appears on *www.blujaiarts.com* and *www.booksxyz.com*. I put a notice of it in my high school alumni magazine and in my college alumni magazine.

I realize that my novel has quite a few different areas of interest, but you need to determine these for your work, and then try and capitalize on them. I also did an interview on Jewish Voice television and several interviews on the radio. I spoke on Jim Hickman's "Wake Up U.S.A.— A UFO Study" on his national radio show with hundreds of listeners who asked questions from a chat room. The interview is now available at *www.mixonic.com*. I also did an interview for my local newspaper and several book signings at local bookstores.

Did any or all of this effort generate book sales? Only time will tell, but I have satisfaction in knowing that I have and will continue to give it my best.

Stephen Yulish is the author of
The Great Harpazo Deception: The Real Story of UFOs

Public Speaking
and Interviews

———————————◆

Steps to a Successful Radio Interview

Maynard Cowan III

Many new authors, published for the first time, find that promoting their work is not as easy as they might have imagined. Many look for professional help, hiring a literary publicist to assist them in their task. This is not necessarily a bad idea, but one that can be very expensive. Thousands of dollars can be spent, with sometimes very disappointing results. Before you decide on that route, consider what you expect a publicist to do for you. Publicists do not sell books. They will promote you to media outlets that may or may not be the right one for your work. You may or may not be received by an audience who is interested in buying your book. So before you part with your hard-earned money, consider how much publicity you can do on your own.

You will first need a good, professional press release. Examples and training are readily available on the Internet. Pressreleasetoolkit.com is an excellent place to start. You will also need a publicity packet. This should include a copy of your book, a personal fact sheet, copies of articles you've written or had published in newspapers or magazines, and a list of possible questions a potential interviewer might want to ask you about your book.

The target of your press release should be local radio talk shows. Your chances of being invited on *Imus in the Morning* are slim, so concentrate on the radio stations that have local shows rather than nationally syndicated programs. Start with your hometown stations first, and then branch out regionally.

You can easily fax or e-mail your press release to hundreds of radio stations that are constantly looking for new guests for their shows. Once you have a response, send the station your publicity packet and then follow up with a phone call to the station to make sure they received your information and to discuss the time you'll be a guest on their show.

Make sure you've read your own book; you'd be surprised how many authors haven't. This way you won't be surprised by a question the talk-show host might ask you that isn't on your list of questions provided in your publicity packet.

The beauty of radio talk shows is that you don't have to travel to do them. Almost every talk show is done via telephone. Make sure you use a landline; cell phones are sometimes not very reliable. Another plus is that you're doing public speaking without the audience staring back at you. Some people are terrified to speak in front of groups. Radio is just you and the show's host having a conversation about your favorite subject, your book.

Before you send out your first press release, make sure your book is readily available. If you've contacted local bookstores, make sure they have an ample supply on hand, because radio does sell books. Consider setting up an 800 number where listeners can call and buy your book right after the show. A personal website where listeners can log on during the show and purchase your book is also a great idea. Most listeners will be compelled to buy your book immediately following your appearance on the show. Make it easy for them to buy it. You'll need a credit card arrangement with your local bank to process credit card sales you make on your 800 number or your personal website.

The main thing to remember when you're a guest on a radio talk show is the title of your book. Mention it as many times as you comfortably are able. No one will be able to buy your book if they don't know its title.

After you've been on several radio talk shows and the royalties are rolling in, then you might consider hiring a professional literary publicist to further enhance your success. My guess is you won't need them.

Maynard Cowan III is the author of *Character Centered Living*

A Broadcaster's Point of View
Tom Elkins

My first book is still several months away from final release, so I have no real-life experiences to pass along. However, I did spend over 40 years in radio and television, as a writer, reporter, anchor, on-air personality, salesman and owner-operator. Perhaps it would help you to understand interviews from a broadcaster's point of view, so you can be better prepared.

First, you should recognize that the nirvana of getting on network television is probably not going to happen. That needn't stop you from trying, but the networks are assaulted daily by thousands who want to peddle their wares free of charge. The odds aren't good, unless you have an angle.

I would recommend starting in your hometown, or the community where your story takes place. From there you might try to branch out to a nearby major city, if you aren't already in one. If you know that a particular on-air personality does interviews, contact that person. Otherwise, ask for the program director. Your pitch should include a reason why talking about your book would be interesting to his/her listeners/viewers. But keep in mind, he/she will be doing you a favor, not vice-versa. He/she already has an audience. On-air people have already succeeded in their media. Ask if he/she would like to read the book, and, if he/she says yes, give him/her a copy.

Being on-the-air can be a daunting experience for people unaccustomed to it. Being nervous is the norm. We all were the first time. Take a deep breath before you go on, and try to focus on the interviewer. He/she is a professional. His/her purpose is not to embarrass you. You may provide him/her with a list of suggested questions, but most good interviewers will come up with their own. For his/her sake, do not answer questions "yes" or "no." Nothing is more frustrating to an interviewer. If he/she asks, "Was the research on this book difficult?" it should start you off on a one- or two-minute reply. Talk to the interviewer, not to the camera or the microphone. It'll help quiet the butterflies. Concentrate on his/her questions and try to be responsive. If you don't know the answer, say, "I don't know, but I'll try to find out."

More than likely, you'll be on radio. Local programming on television is in short supply these days. When you're doing a radio interview, keep in mind that the listener can't see you. A nod of the head, a shrug or a hand gesture doesn't transmit. You won't be able to show your book cover; you, or the interviewer, will have to describe it. Briefly. "It's the brown book with the cowboy on the cover" would be good, presuming that describes your book.

The interviewer's purpose is to provide something interesting to his/her audience. Your purpose is to sell your book. Ideally, you should both accomplish your goals. If he/she doesn't ask, "and where can our listeners buy your book?" toward the end, you might prompt him/her, "is it alright if I tell your listeners where they can get the book?" And be ready with the information.

Of course, this assumes your book is released and can be purchased right away. Don't go for an interview before that time. Listeners' memories are short.

And…good luck!

Tom Elkins is the author of *North of Texas*

Public Speaking Among Howling Wolves

Ray Austin Kampa

Not too long ago, The Book of Lists organization performed a survey on the top 10 fears that people have. Number one was the fear of public speaking. The full list follows:

1) Speaking before a group
2) Heights
3) Insects and bugs
4) Financial problems
5) Deep water
6) Sickness
7) Death
8) Flying
9) Loneliness
10) Dogs

What makes public speaking so fearful, even more terrifying than death? One thing that happens is a physical reaction which is exactly the same as stage fright: Your adrenaline kicks in — your palms get sweaty, your heart rate rises, your mind seems to lock, and you wish you could crawl into a hole and hide. This is a natural reaction to the fear of being captured, killed, and eaten by a pack of wild animals, perhaps howling wolves. Yet we know that the people who make up an audience are humans just like us, and generally speaking, few cannibals are to be found in any given audience.

Yet, we have this instinctual fear. Some people seem to give an oral presentation as if it were the easiest thing in the world to do; however, almost every one of these people have had to face their natural reactions and learn the skills to control them. This control leads to turning emotion into positive energy during performances. If you feel a natural fear of public speaking, as most people do, take heart that you can also take control. All that is required is to understand the techniques to do this and to practice the techniques. Several books are on the market addressing this issue, and the following website will give you a start on how you can practice public speaking in a supportive environment: www.toastmasters.org

Toastmasters International has been in existence for many years. The website will give you information on chapters in your area.

While in college, I had the grand opportunity to hear the author of *Lord Grizzly*, Frederick Manfred, speak about the novel and his writing process. What impressed me as a student of both English and speech was his relaxed approach. He moved easily from behind the podium and approached us in a way that hinted if we had been in a smaller setting, he'd have been walking and talking among us. This is an especially good technique for public speaking, one worth emulating, and also the hardest to master. While your instincts want to get this all over with as quickly as possible, your mind needs to exercise its dominance over emotion in order to pace the thoughts, keep the delivery clear, and maintain a thread of coherence all the way through.

One way I have found that works well in all settings is to imagine that you're talking with a good friend. Being a writer, this should not be too much of an imagination stretch for you. Try looking in a mirror and practice your speaking while imagining that the image looking back at you is your best friend. Alternatively, try talking to a photo of your best friend or even ask if you can practice your speaking directly with him or her. Then take special note of how you feel while doing this. Actually, it may take a few sessions to completely relax into the comfortable state that you're trying to feel, since talking in a self-conscious mode to a best friend can also be stressful. But that's what you want. You want to get past self-consciousness, feel the comfort and remember it, possibly visualizing your friend's face while speaking in public.

Here's another thing that works: Practice hand, arm, body, and facial expressions. Walk around while talking, but don't pace back and forth. Try to stop moving at appropriate times to emphasize points or to place a pause between main ideas. We writers know how to use commas and other punctuation to do this in our prose — think of your motions as punctuation marks while speaking.

Observing and commenting on other speakers' performances can help you to develop a style that is uniquely yours, just as you've developed a unique style of writing from reading many other authors. You may want to incorporate the techniques of others in your presentation style, or you may witness things that you want to avoid. For example, I find the antics of many politicians to be annoying, and so I avoid the use of a clenched fist with a thumb sticking up and random karate chops in the air. On the other hand, I've picked up some valuable ideas from actors playing politicians in movies. Part of this learning process is to pay attention to the fine details of delivery, and who can better display this than professional actors?

I'm the first person to admit that stage fright is a real and common problem for those of us who are called upon to do public speaking every so often. Part of the reason I minored in speech was to rise above this problem, but I found that it never goes away. Still, what the butterflies amount to is an excited energy that can be controlled, directed, and used to give more interesting presentations. This takes practice, and a good way to start is with a mirror, photograph, or best friend. Once you've felt a degree of comfort and practiced going into that comfortable place, then using Toastmasters International for live experiences in a supportive setting can help you to achieve what Frederick Manfred displayed to me in his presentation.

Ray Austin Kampa is the author of *Deer in the Headlamps*

Having a Good Time
Selling Books
Louise S. MacDonald

Though I did not have success in e-mailing newspaper editors and reviewers, talk show hosts and TV stations, I realized that my two books, derived from my eight-year residence in Morocco as a foreign correspondent, might prove interesting and informative to ordinary people as they strove to deal with the trauma caused by the events of 9/11/01. I would talk about my experiences living among and writing about Muslims.

At first I searched the local phone books for women's clubs, then I went online at Google.com and found over 20 lesser-known women's clubs in Baltimore and suburban towns surrounding both Baltimore and Washington D.C., all within an hour or so drive from my home. My letter promoted my book, spoke of its timeliness and included a short resume of my career as a reporter/writer and foreign correspondent. A lot of correspondence ensued, proving that some clubs were defunct and others did not have programs at their meetings. However, most clubs answered in the positive, asking if I charged an honorarium. I had decided that I would not start with an honorarium, hoping to sell books at a signing after my talk. (Later, I began to charge $50 for talks.) I gave the clubs' program directors a choice of subject matter: a) living among the Muslims b) my career from reporter to foreign correspondent, c) Islam: belief, customs and lifestyle, d) a travel talk on Morocco with slides e) the war in the Sahara (which I had covered as the only American and the only woman).

Because my subject matter is timely and cogent, I received very positives responses via e-mail. In the end, I talked to a total of 15 different women's clubs, to a senior educational group and to the prestigious Explorers' Club in Washington. I have spoken to two church groups. Since I also write poetry,

I read my work at three poetry gatherings. As I am a docent at the Baltimore Museum of Art, I held an art show of docents' work in my home and sold many books. I also contacted two book groups and sold all the members copies of my books. My talks lasted from twenty minutes to one hour, however long the club program director wanted me to speak, and took place after a luncheon or evening meeting. Afterwards, the question-and-answer period went on for another fifteen minutes, at least. All of the programs went very well and were followed by enthusiastic questions and comments. I received gifts and flowers — and I sold a lot of books! At one occasion, set up at the last minute for the Maryland Federation of Women's Clubs, I didn't have enough books with me to meet the demand! Sometimes I sold few books, but I felt that the effort was worth it because of the importance of my message of tolerance and understanding of Muslims who, for the most part, are peace-loving individuals whose normal lives do not differ greatly from our own.

So far I have spoken to 25 groups and have sold hundreds of copies of my books. I am continuing to appear at various types of gatherings. Although I stuttered somewhat as a child, my experience as a museum docent had accustomed me to public speaking and I soon found that I was not shy about it at all, and that I actually enjoyed my "performances" a great deal and met many wonderful people. Believe me, many groups of people who meet regularly are looking for speakers to tell them interesting and insightful tales of their experiences.

Louise S. MacDonald (Louise Roberts Sheldon) is the author of *Wind in the Sahara* and *Casablanca Notebook*.

Having Fun with Public Speaking

J.P. Maynard

I'd like to emphasize that talking to others about your book is *fun*. There is no reason at all to feel shy or nervous. People are genuinely curious about writers and their work.

I have particularly enjoyed talking to small groups about my books. One such instance comes to mind where everyone had an especially good time.

I had been asked by a local Ruritan club to talk about a book that had recently come out; it had as one of its themes a stock swindle. Beforehand, I printed on my computer some very official-looking stock certificates, with a blank line to be filled in with the name of a new share owner. Before I started to talk, I gave a certificate to each one of the twenty so present and then acted out a very obvious snake-oil spiel: "Ladies and gentlemen, if you want to become filthy rich, all it takes is a minute investment of $50 a share…" And went on from there, amidst much laughter.

Afterwards, I questioned them: "How would you feel if you had succumbed to my sales talk, bought some stock, and later found it to be worthless?" We went around and around on that for a good fifteen minutes. It was an enjoyable time.

I only sold a couple of books that evening because just about everyone present had already bought a copy, and then brought them to me to autograph. But I'm sure their subsequent talking to others about the meeting resulted in further sales.

J. P. Maynard is the author of *The Murderous Bride*

A Tentative Speech for My Book Promotion

Gary L. Palmer

Getting a book published is not an easy task, especially a first book, but it's not brain surgery. First and foremost, the writer has to be an optimist; a writer's chances of getting struck by lightning are greater than his or her chances of getting a book published. Winston Churchill spoke eloquently about optimism: "The pessimist sees the difficulty in every opportunity; the optimist sees the opportunity in every difficulty."

Secondly, the writer has to become an expert in three areas: revision, perseverance, and research. He or she must revise, revise, and revise; if need be, every word, every sentence, and every paragraph, many times over. The search for the proper placement and the best words for each sentence must be ongoing. Mark Twain was a master at finding the right word; he stated his intentions so aptly when he said: "The difference between the right word and the not so right word is the difference between lightning and the lightning bug."

Perseverance goes without saying; it's the key to success in any endeavor. In 1995, two years after I began writing my book, I started sending query letters to agents, editors, and publishing houses. My optimistic nature had me believing that my project would be of interest to many. Was I ever mistaken; the form rejection letters came rushing in like Christmas cards in December. Reality had set in, and humility quickly followed. I questioned myself about my ambition to be a writer: Do the piles of rejection letters mean I can't write well, or do they mean I can't write well, yet?

Since I have always enjoyed writing, I decided to keep trying until I got it right. It's like learning to ride a bicycle, hit a baseball, or target practice with a rifle. You simply get better my doing it over and over and over again. During his presidency, John Quincy Adams said, "Patience and perseverance have a magical effect before which difficulties disappear and obstacles vanish." And the legendary Woody Hayes used to say, "Nothing worthwhile comes easy."

But one thing did come easy: Finding and liking challenges. I have especially taken to heart three quotes about those that doubt rather than act. Eleanor Roosevelt said, "Believe in yourself. You must do what people think you cannot do." Walter Bagehot, a nineteenth-century British author, banker, and social reformer spoke in similar terms when he said, "The greatest pleasure in life is doing what people say you cannot do." And Shakespeare's words in *Measure For Measure* have echoed through the centuries, "Our doubts are traitors, and make us lose the good we oft might win, by fearing to attempt."

The third necessary ingredient to becoming an author is research. I learned at a writers' conference that historical events should be mixed into memoirs; it gives the readers a sense of the time period. Through research I was able to "spot-in" many historical events that I had either forgotten about, or never knew in the first place. Also, research became a tool to authenticate dates, places, and happenings that I hadn't previously researched. Research is also needed to find literary agents, editors, publishing houses, writers' conferences, local writers' clubs, and the best magazines for writers. Lastly, research, more than anything, usually determines a writer's fate; it did mine. I discovered PublishAmerica through Internet research. Regardless of genre, research is a writer's best friend. Pulitzer Prize-winning author, David McCullough, had this to say about research: "I'm still researching right up until the last page, and I'm still researching things I've already written about."

My tenth-grade English teacher, Mrs. Hensley, can be credited with my start in writing. Every six-weeks grading period, our assignment was to read a book, and either turn in a written book report, or do the unthinkable, give an oral report in front of the class. I never read a book the entire year, but I always turned in handwritten book reports. My made-up stories were always about brave and adventurous people, or sports heroes. My grades on the book reports during that memorable 1955-56 school year ranged from B plus to C minus, enabling me to skate through English with my typical grade of C, surpassed only by my grades in gym class and geometry. To this day, I'm not sure if Mrs. Hensley was fooled by my fake stories and fake authors, or decided to "play the game" to enhance my creativity.

My creative non-fiction first book took a lot longer than my fictitious English themes. *Chagrin Falls* was accepted for publication after nine years of writing. It had three different names, two genres, was rewritten 16 times, and revised more times than I have been able to keep track. It was an autobiography for eight years before becoming a memoir. Another Pulitzer Prize-winning author, Frank McCourt, describes a memoir: "A memoir is a segment of your life, seen through your eyes." An autobiography, also written in the first person, covers an entire lifetime.

My editor, Susan, whom I met at a writers' conference, is credited for naming my book, and changing it from an autobiography to a memoir. She was an instructor, and my reader and manuscript evaluator at the conference. Susan has a Ph.D. from Columbia University, and is a published author. She writes essays and memoirs for the *Philadelphia Enquirer* and *The Hudson Review*, teaches college creative-writing classes, and wrote the first published biography of Flannery O'Connor. Not only is she credited with changing the genre, and renaming my book, but also her intuitive skills helped me to understand my characters, including myself, a lot better. I'll never forget what she wrote on my hard copy after she had read about the day my parents abandoned my brothers and me: "Gary, what were your feelings; what were you thinking? The readers have to know how you felt during these trying times in your life." Susan's total package of editing skills were a big factor in getting my book published.

And then there's the person who has helped me the most to become a better writer, my wife of 35 years, Barbara. An avid reader, she noticed some of the same things that Susan noticed: poor transition; not enough description of my personal feelings, and use of the five senses; and lastly, statements, paragraphs and events that were out of sequence. Barb also noticed something else: "You can't tell all; you have to let the reader use their imagination and draw conclusions."

Would I have gotten a book published without an editor like Susan, and a wife as helpful as Barbara? Whoops! There I go again, trying to tell it all again.

Gary L. Palmer is the author of *Chagrin Falls*

We Don't Do it for the Money
Jim Roper

Effective promotion should flow easily from the same powerful motivation that gave life to your book. The primary reason I wrote two military memoirs was to remember fallen brothers. *Quoth the Raven* introduces wonderful people who gave all doing the same job to which I gave a year in Vietnam and Laos. I believe no one dies until he is forgotten.

Ego drove the second reason — to carve a little slice of earthly immortality. Third, I felt challenged when critics rightfully bashed my early scribbling. Fourth, the story ran around inside my head like a hungry dog. It refused to be suppressed. I like money, but you won't find it high on this list.

If your motivations emerge as clearly as mine do, your next step only involves mechanics. Attach that engine to your plan. If you aren't as simply driven, you may have to reflect and find the prime reason you put pen to paper. Do the Maui thing.

A good promotion plan includes book signings. Booksellers like authors, but they ask for several months of lead-time to set up a signing. Four months seems like a long period, but I have found real-world needs of the day job, family, and that next book make time the hardest commodity to grasp.

Immediately after handing the bookstore manager a signed book and a press release for her newsletter, I set up speeches and local talk-radio appearances. I posted signs and brochures promoting the signing. And I worked on Ropersbooks.com. No one ever called me a computer genius.

Service clubs, libraries, and organizations relating to your book's theme welcome guest speakers. These groups provide receptive audiences, and they respect the difficult task of creating a book. Prepare well. I could extemporize for hours about my books. Twenty minutes requires practice. Mark Twain said that first.

I approach each organization confidently, remembering that my story will help create another generation of life for my friends who did not survive

Vietnam. See how I'm tying this theory together?

Passing along the story also increases my chances for immortality, so I take my best shot. For people who like lists, here come my speaking secrets:

1. Learn something about the group before you show up. For instance, I always thank Kiwanians for helping children worldwide. They deserve it. You will make new friends.

2. If you are a critique group veteran, offer to help any budding writers in the audience by editing their first twenty pages. You owe this to the system of folks who helped you reach the publishable level. Also, this will justify your leaving brochures or business cards with your contact information.

3. Tell them something they never heard before. I might start with: "During the Vietnam War, the United States lost four hundred and ninety-three airplanes over Laos. And Laos was a neutral country." Leave time for questions.

If you squeeze the most from time, you may need to recharge your batteries. Attend a writers' conference. Re-read those "How to Market Yourself" books. Network. The most successful author who has helped you might be your best source for media appearances.

Good luck. But believing the proverb that luck arrives at the intersection of preparation and opportunity, I might better suggest, get busy!

Jim Roper is the author of *Quoth the Raven* and *Aardvarks and Rangers*

Tips on Public Speaking
George W. Spence

Although I can't speak from experience as an author presenting a work in public, I can speak from experience as a pulpit preacher and as a nursing-home speaker. Can't be a whole lot different, can they? I studied public speaking in college and the lessons I learned there applied to the church venue.

I controlled my nervousness by believing what I was saying, by knowing what I was talking about and by being prepared. If you don't believe what you're saying, you will not convince your audience either. You'll be able to see it on their faces. If you don't know what you're talking about, you'll come across as a fool and your listeners will know it. If you're not prepared, you'll ramble and stumble and your nervousness will give you heart palpitations.

Believe in your subject matter, learn all you can about it and prepare, prepare, prepare! Don't try to memorize a speech verbatim, but prepare an outline and practice, practice, practice what you want to say. Use your outline to keep yourself on track and to get back to the subject if someone steers you away from it. Forget about visualizing everyone in your audience sitting there naked — it doesn't work and it can be a distraction. If looking straight into someone's eyes is difficult for you, try looking at a spot just above the head of a person behind him as you move your gaze about. You'll appear to have eye contact and you won't be quite so nervous.

Georger W. Spence is the author of *A Season for Everything*

Book
Signings

♦

You are a Walking, Talking Advertisement for Your Book!
Chris Cole and Cody Lee (C.C. Colee)

Have you ever stood in line at the store and heard the person in front of you mention wanting a good book to read? Ever have someone you haven't seen in a while come up to you and ask "Well, what have you been doing with yourself lately?" Are you prepared with your answer? Is it going to just be words?

No, never let it be just words! As you are speaking about being a published author, or how you have your book in production, find that handout to pass along. It could be a brochure that can easily be made using many different computer programs. It can be a business card or bookmark. We have seen business cards that have the author name with "AUTHOR" underneath and the e-mail address. Okay, that's fine, but the author of what? Make sure that you have your book title and ISBN printed on anything you give out.

We have participated in several book signings at bookstores, but what we have found to be a great deal of fun is being a part of book fair or multi-author book event. Yet, with all of the other authors, and the fun of exchanging experiences and tricks of the trade, you must also remember that you want to stand out and be different from them when the customers start milling around. What can you do to be remembered over the other authors present at the event?

There are all kinds of ways that you can promote your story with hands-on and visualization tools. You have a very creative imagination. If not, then how did you write your book in the first place? Use that creativity to bring your story to life on the display table and let it work for you in your advertising.

As an example, here's what we do. We dress up as the two main female characters in our pirate trilogy, complete with high boots, a sword dangling from the side of the gold sash worn by the captain, and the pirate garb worn by the heroine.

In speaking of using hands-on things to promote your books, we have found that an interesting display will draw folks to your table. We have scattered piratical things of interest on our table, such as a long glass, tankards, goblets, ship models, weaponry, and so on. As each book of our pirate trilogy was released, we added items to our table display that the reader would find in our story. Not only will a person see the piratical paraphernalia, but he/she will also find small items, such as the heroine's ring mentioned throughout the story, and a necklace mentioned in the third book after a plunder.

We have found that our chocolate "doubloons" in a small treasure chest are quite the lure for kids. Sometimes, the kids will spot the candy, ask mom, dad, grandma, grandpa, whomever, if they can have one. When the attention of the adult is drawn by the child to the candy, they begin to see things on our table that draw their interest. We have had many an adults' eyes light up at the sight of chocolate, and they take a couple pieces and strike up a conversation.

Props draw the eye of the folks wandering by, even the ones who patrol amid the tables at a distance of six to eight feet. Something on the table might catch their eye because they are interested in that type of object, or because it is just so intriguing that it calls out for them to come closer and see better. Once they come into that space of about three feet out, you can catch their attention with your friendly hello, or "do you like," and then, of course, you would name the type of items you are displaying. For us, it is a question of "do you like pirates?" or "are you interested in nautical things?"

Now that you have their attention, offer them a brochure, a page of your review(s), a business card or a bookmark, whatever it is that you brought as "carry-off" advertising. You may not make the sale right then and there, but, although it may be disheartening, don't fret. Book fairs can be pretty sensory overwhelming for some folks. A great deal of the time, they come in with one thing or subject in mind. For most, they are generally working with a spending budget when they come.

However, with that one little piece of treasure that you have given them that day, and your smile and conversation, you could make an impression on them that will entice them to check you out a little later, and buy your book online. Sometimes, they come back around the horn the second time, after finding some more change in their little purses, and buy a book on the spot!

At any rate, YOUR information is with them. If they don't use it, they may pass it on to a family member or friend who might be interested. So, you have given them something to think about in your paperwork and you have given them a saleable mental image of you to take home as well. For example, recently we received an e-mail from a woman who has completed reading our trilogy. She writes, "*I saw your booth during the Gasparilla in Tampa Bay, but I didn't realize it was the two of you until my aunt gave me your website address. I was looking through pictures and I saw you with your book display...and thought 'Oh my God, that WAS THEM.'*"

What an adventure it was to write your book, but, friends, the grandest adventure is yet to come. Happy writing and best of luck to you all!

Chris Cole and Cody Lee (C.C. Colee) are the authors of the RB Trilogy—*RB: The Widow Maker*, *RB: The Enchantress*, *RB: The Game*

Communication is the Key
Eugene M. Gagliano

I discovered early that communication is the key to successful book signings. First, I get people's attention by wearing an authentic 1890 shirt, vest, and derby because my middle-grade historical fiction mystery entitled *Secret of the Black Widow* takes place during that time period. Then, I greet people warmly and sincerely with a handshake or a smile, and introduce myself as a Wyoming author. Next, I invite them to enjoy a piece of candy from the basket on my signing table, which sits next to a bright and informative poster about me and my books. Finally, I encourage them to sign up for the raffle of one of my favorite books, some art supplies, or western souvenir, which I provide. I try to get to know a little about the people while they sign up.

If I make the potential buyer feel comfortable and establish a positive rapport, I feel successful. Even if the person doesn't buy a book, at least I have made a positive impression, and perhaps the next time they see me they will make a purchase.

Eugene M. Gagliano is the author of *Secret of the Black Widow* and
Inside the Clown

A New Twist on the Backyard BBQ

Paul Richard

When my first book, *John Tinker's Revenge*, came out, I made about 100 postcards with the cover picture (a gunman) on the front, and details on the back. They were concerning a signing party to be held in our backyard on a certain date. Fortunately, the book came out in the summer. I then mailed the postcards to all my friends, business acquaintances, neighbors, etc., and approximately 75 individuals turned out for the party. We arranged for food and drinks, and I had several boxes of books, which I sold and signed.

Paul Richard is the author of *John Tinker's Revenge* and *The Bird Killer*

Unconventional Book Signings
Dennis Royer

A prime objective for new authors is to gain exposure and generate sales by arranging book signings and having booksellers stock their books. We dream of walking into bookstores and seeing racks displaying multiple copies of our titles. Some of us are fortunate enough to realize this dream, while others of us meet with stiff resistance from bookstore management.

Consider that during 2002, a whopping 150,000 new US titles and editions were released. Of this, 17,000 fell under the category of general adult fiction.[1] Do the math. If each of these publications has a spine that averages 1-inch thick, the total new shelf space required to stock just 1 copy of each new general adult fiction book would be over a quarter mile. Given these numbers, as a bookstore manager, what would you stock? In such a competitive environment, management is going to opt for what they know will sell. As unknowns, we are pushed aside to make way for the latest Rowling, King, Grisham, Koontz, and Roberts. How can we compete with these big names for precious bookstore shelf space?

My strategy is this: If I'm not welcome at bookstores, I'll go where I'm wanted. By doing so, it is possible to generate just as much noise and publicity as a conventional bookstore book signing. Here is how it is working for me.

Restaurants — I recently approached the owner of a neighborhood family-run restaurant about hosting a book signing. This owner was very receptive at the prospect of having "a local, famous author" appear. We agreed to do this on a Tuesday evening to generate increased traffic for the restaurant on what is typically a slow night. The owner also agreed to display my book at the cash register and sell copies in advance of the signing. I prepared a press release, which resulted in a prominent announcement in our local newspaper and a separately published article and photo-op about my book and me. Eight copies were purchased at the restaurant before the event, and I sold another ten during the signing. What pleased me most was not just the number of books sold, but the buzz created by the publicity and from all of the customers that told their family and friends.

Libraries — I found that most public libraries have someone in the position equivalent to an "events manager" and that they are eager to host signings. Not many sales resulted from this one, but another announcement appeared in the newspaper, thus sustaining the buzz. I also managed to sell two copies to the library for general circulation.

Local Government Meetings — I must admit that I work for a school district, so news of my book quickly caught the attention of the superintendent of schools. You can just as easily contact the secretary for your superintendent, and make known your situation. Most government meetings have as part of their agenda a time set aside for public recognition of noteworthy events. I agreed to appear at a local school-board meeting to discuss my achievement. A spontaneous book signing occurred after the meeting! Here is another tip: There is always at least one newspaper reporter at government meetings. For me, this resulted in another article and a photo-op in a different newspaper.

Local Arts' Councils — I arranged for the local arts' council to display and sell my book in their gallery. There is also a future book signing planned — another opportunity for newspaper publicity.

Book Clubs — Because of the above-mentioned school-board meeting, I was invited to appear as a guest author at a local book club. I signed everyone's copy after answering their questions, and one of the members posted a very kind review on Amazon.com in the name of the book club.

In the near future, I will once again approach bookstore managers. This time, I will be armed with a portfolio of recent newspaper announcements, feature articles, and a book-club review. In the manager's eyes, will this make me as popular as Rowling or King? Maybe not, but I can now present a strong case that I have risen above most of the other 17,000 newly published fiction authors.

Dennis Royer is the author of *Stranger*

---

[1] "U.S. Book Production Tops 150,000 in 2002," News Release, http://www.bowker.com/bowkerweb/Press_Releases/DecadeBookProd.htm, May 26, 2003

New and Foreign Perspectives

———————————————◆

Coming Soon!
Josephine Davis

I just received word in April 2003, of my acceptance into the PublishAmerica family of authors. I do not know when my book, *Healing Poems from the Heart* will be published, but I created a "Coming Soon!" publicity website. It has brought positive results and I have a following that grows each day. In addition, I had business cards made advertising the site. I give them out at appropriate locales; bookstores, people I meet, friends and relatives.

The community relations director at Barnes & Noble has asked that I contact her again when my book is available and others have asked for extra cards so that they may pass them along to their circle of acquaintances. Everyone has had good wishes for me and I will update my website periodically with future developments.

Josephine Davis is the author of *Healing Poems from the Heart*

Keep Daydreaming!
Linda Doty

I am still getting used to the idea of being a published author, while I wait in blissful anticipation of seeing my first children's book, *In Search of the Robin*, in print. My advice is to keep daydreaming. Remember when you were in school and the teacher would call out your name and ask, "Are you daydreaming again?" It happened to me many times while growing up. Sometimes it was just better to block out the real world and escape. I know now that all my daydreaming was the writer in me trying to get out. Just as the writer daydreams past the pile of rejection letters, seeing himself as a published author.

Now it is time to daydream again. See yourself successfully promoting your book. Visualize yourself going to library readings and bookstore signings. As you do this, you will get from your own creative imagination the information you need to help you promote yourself in the best possible way.

For example, I was daydreaming that I was at a book signing at a local library. I imagined a woman came up to me and told me she was a bird watcher and loved my book, *In Search of the Robin*. This gave me the idea to send a press release out to all the bird-watcher magazines and the Audubon Society. So the daydream gave me some very helpful information.

So, writers, keep daydreaming!

Linda Doty is the author of *In Search of the Robin*

Take a Tip from Honest Abe
Charles Haislip

On this subject I cannot speak from experience, as I have not yet had a book released. I do have some ideas, though, that may be helpful that I would like to pass on. I believe each time we have an election for any kind of public office the same type of promotional ideas are displayed that a published author should heed for his/her own promotional guidelines.

* Business cards
* Any chances of public exposure: speaker at special events, book signing, TV or radio interviews, talk shows, etc.
* Create your own webpage, and keep it updated. You know yourself, let the public know you.
* Sometimes it might seem degrading to blow your own horn, so whenever it's possible, let your friends or relatives take care of this for you.
* Try to create some type of fan club.
* Last but not least, if you know of any other authors in your area, try getting together and talking a little strategy.

Abraham Lincoln, to make himself seem more important, dropped letters from his pocket, supposedly written by very prominent and influential people, that were actually written by himself.

Daniel Boone, in promoting himself as an outdoorsman and hunter, carved his name and the date of killing a bear on a certain tree. This all could be very true, but were there any witnesses?

Let your mind wonder for a while, see what happens.

Charles Haislip is the author of *Escape from Bliss*

Put in the Extra Effort

Lura Jackowski

I'm a new author, and as a new author, I am just getting a taste of the promotional end of being published. I found that book stores aren't quick to do signings, but if you can find one that still does, you can usually pick up a couple of sales that you wouldn't have gotten otherwise. Library signings pick up the friends of friends and people you haven't met yet.

Find some friends at distance that can get the word out to friends you don't know. Go to school with your children and talk to their class. Find someone traveling that would give it a read in public to draw attention to the cover; at least it may be remembered when seen again elsewhere.

And when you think you are done, go back out and drop some consignments at gift shops and airports. People are more willing to help you sell if they get something out of their time without it costing them initially, so this works well with split-upon sales, if you're willing to give it time. Also, when it starts getting tough, pass a couple promotional books to friends that sit at an office desk or public place where they can set it on a desk or counter — when they aren't reading it! — so others can see it and get curious about whether it is a good read. Some even spend their days in malls sitting at a table waiting for the people passing by to talk to them in hopes they may sell a book.

It takes time to sell something new. So always remember a published author has seven years to sell it well enough in order to re-sign to sell it some more. It's worth the effort to see your works out there, and it's a good feeling when people recognize you as an author.

Lura Jackowski is the author of *Rainbow Dreams* and
Vacation Rainbow

YOU Are Your Most Powerful Tool

Niki Mylonas

When PublishAmerica approached me for a contribution detailing my endeavors in promoting *myself* as a "published author," I froze! Not quite able to call myself a *published* author yet, as my first book is undergoing the publishing process as I write, what on earth could I say to others? Nevertheless, I've managed to salvage a few tips and some positive ways of thinking, which might help *you* to get on in the ruthless world of the creative arts. Here is what I've thought about, done, and achieved, and how my efforts have paid off.

I've swallowed my modesty, put myself in top gear and "taken the bull by its horns" in order to come up with this piece of, hopefully, useful and philosophical advice. To my surprise, I've discovered I'm quite skillful when it comes to "selling" myself as an author. The number-one rule to remember is to be *resourceful* and rely on *you* as a talented artist. CONFIDENCE and AUDACITY are the *key* ingredients of spurning one on to approach the great doors of success! Once you've decided to GO, just knock — LOUDLY!

Apart from a mailing list I submitted to my publisher, and spreading the word to friends and acquaintances, I assumed that once a publishing house accepted my "baby," I could relax! And without any further input from me, as its creator, the book would sell. I'd make plenty of money, give up my day job, and continue to produce literature and live comfortably forevermore! Thus, I didn't think I had to do *anything* else to get noticed.

WRONG!

This was the BIGGEST mistake I made as a young actress when I first left drama school. Although I applied for work, I wasn't pushy enough. I rarely followed anything up afterwards. I didn't "chase up" the work, or the people who were in the positions to give me roles. I assumed that the work would find *me*. Hence, *complacency* was an easy cushion to collapse into. This is *hazardous!* You really can't afford to take it easy at this stage, because you have to become *established* before you can work at your own pace and earn "proper" money.

It was my *publisher* who made me aware of the work that still needs to be dealt with, even *after* the finished product hits the bookstore shelves! If you are just starting out, many people would not have heard of you or know of your work and the *only* way of making yourself known is to put *yourself* about! After all, you've written a masterpiece, haven't you? You want to share it with the *world,* not just with local people or friends? You want to *make a living* out of being creatively gifted? Then, the answer is plain and simple — get *out* there and *talk* to people who are in the know and in the industry! Visit bookshops, book fairs, libraries, colleges, schools, and both magazine and newspaper houses! DON'T be despondent if the latter two don't listen the first time around, they soon will if you are persistent enough!

I have done *all* the above in less than a handful of weeks, and although, I'm still waiting to hear from my local newspapers and magazines, I have had some positive results from local independent bookshops, some of the large chain booksellers and my local library!

Booksellers, to my knowledge, are intelligent people who have always been approachable and delighted to be of assistance. My local bookshops were more than happy to hear of new writing material by a local author and welcomed flyers for display! One has even agreed to stock some copies and give me 25% of the profits! This would mean that *I* would have to purchase the books first, however, which is not ideal, but if that is what it takes to get my foot in the door, then so be it!

The large chain bookstores usually purchase books from representatives, and I've found out that *I,* as an author, can act as a rep for my own book. I just have to arrange an appointment.

My local librarian, Gwen, was a rock. I could display a flyer on the main notice board and she could book me into the timetable to hold a "talk," which would include readings of my work. I could even sell copies on that day. I felt nervous at the thought of talking to a room full of people as *myself,* but there's a first time for everything, and I would just have to do it if I want to get on! Answer? GO FOR IT!

Most booksellers and libraries purchase their literature via suppliers, who, in turn, have to obtain "rights" before they buy material! Unfortunately, the people I spoke to were not at liberty to disclose the identity of those suppliers. I was hoping I could persuade *them* to purchase my work from my American publisher! If you are able to obtain such information, you're a step ahead!

When I attended the last book fair in London, I felt a little modest in approaching some of the stallholders. MISTAKE! You are *only* intimidated if you *allow* yourself to be! Be BOLD! Chances are, they *could* be interested.

Your book could benefit students. Contacting colleges with your subject would be worthwhile. If it's a good and informative book, it will be recommended for *years*.

My main difficulty as a published author is to break into the market in England, where I live. I'm honored that America has plucked me from obscurity and taken a huge gamble. If the States has faith in me as a writer, then so should my *own* people!

There is much work to be done! Remember — DON'T SIT BACK! Your publisher has laid the *main* foundation; *YOU* are your most powerful tool in this business because *YOU* are the creator of your book!

Niki Mylonas is the author of *Wide Eyes – Memories of a Childhood, Autobiographical Stories of Experience, Thought & Observation*

Whenever, Wherever

David M. Seymon

I am a newcomer to the ranks in this portion of the writing market. I do have a few ideas concerning bringing my book to the public's eye. Whenever I am out, wherever I am, whomever I am with, I tell people about my book.

1. Should I be in line at a store, bank, doctor's office — it really does not matter — I talk about my new book as if it was the hottest thing to come across the pike.

2. I always carry business cards with the book title, my name, type of story it is, and where to purchase my fine book, *www.publishamerica.com.*

3. When it is appropriate, I take a copy of my book and show the potential customer(s) my work. (As we know, actions speak louder than words, or a book in the hand is worth….)

Those are a few of my ploys to interest the possible buyer. All they can say is that they do not like to read. Although I am brain damaged, I shake their hand and tell them how much I appreciated their listening to me and walk to the next person or group of purchasers.

David M. Seymon is the author of *Reflections of Gratitude*

A Non-American Perspective
Harry Simenon

You have just finished your first book, and even found a publisher. The only thing left to do is to find someone to buy your book!

Although friends and family will buy your work, they will usually do this because it is your book, not because they like the story. Most of them will never even read it! So they will not rave about the story to their friends, they will only tell that their friend or relative wrote a book! I expect that this will not lead to many sales.

There is only one reason for buying the work of an unknown writer: The story must appeal to people. And to make this happen, they must know about its existence, of course.

Promoting is more difficult for non-American writers like me, for practical reasons:

* A plane ticket and hotel stay are more expensive than a car trip, and usually more time consuming.

* Nobody knows you; there is no hometown where you can stimulate people personally.

* Only few books will sell in your country, as your book is usually not written in your language. Actually, the total market would be much smaller if you would have written it in your own language.

* It is not easy to find out about contacts to obtain a critique about your book.

So electronic book selling is the main way to work. Most readers will not be very different from writers. Think of what makes you buy a book. I usually read the synopsis to find out if the topic is of any interest to me; after that, I start reading the first chapter. If I forget the time, I'll buy it.

The same thing should apply for electronic shopping. I will not buy a book, having read solely the synopsis; I like to taste the style of story telling.

This is why I think it is a good idea to produce a webpage (this is not difficult at all anymore), and make the first chapter of your book available for reading. This way you can give people a chance to find out if your book is worth their money. At the end of the chapter, you can make a link to the publisher, so they can purchase the book.

Some people use the old "page hundred" trick. Usually, the first pages of a book have seen many revisions; the writer knows that these pages are very important to hook the reader, and spends a lot time perfecting them. The more clever book buyers open the book at page hundred; if this page has the same quality as the first pages, they consider it to be worth buying. The writer never knows which page will end up being page hundred when going into print, so this is a good method. Maybe it is possible to let the reader choose to read one other page outside the first chapter, to allow them to be able to judge the quality of the book. One possibility is to e-mail a page at request.

This will not help the ill-written books, but personally I think this will be an advantage. It will force writers to do the best they can, and convince buyers it is safe to order books you have only seen on the Internet. Bad books never serve the long-term market.

Another problem is, of course, to guide people to your website, outside the usual admittance to browsers. One thing I planned to do is to print coasters advertising the website and offer them to literary pubs. The problem is that, although these pubs are abundant in Europe, there are not that many in the USA, it seems. Non-literary pubs might still work. Printing coasters is also quite expensive!

Harry Simenon is the author of *The Barren Grounds*

Utilizing Outside Knowledge
Steve Stevich

While I'm new to the book industry, I have experience in a lot of the fields pertaining to marketing products. To get started, you want to talk with radio announcers, disc jockies, etc. to get on their shows. That will open the public to acquire knowledge of who you are, and could lead to possible television interviews.

With some public interviews behind you, you can call bookstores to set up a book signing and publicity day at the store. You can put a large poster in the book store window announcing the day of your visit.

Public speaking is a learned process. I suggest you tape yourself speaking, and learn your weaknesses in your presentation abilities from what the tape shows. I did that 40-some years ago and have talked to well over 300,000+ people; I stopped counting in 1980 when I reached 80,000 people. The experience teaches you impromptu responses to either friendly or hostile questions from the audience.

As far as nervousness, well I have always been nervous before going on stage. That gets your adrenalin flowing; for if it doesn't, you will be a dull speaker. As you begin to speak, you can actually mentally and spiritually leave the stage and go out into the audience and mingle with them as you speak. I say being nervous is normal and you need to be before going out on stage to speak. If you get so uptight you get sick, then I suggest you start small by standing before your family and giving a speech. Once done, you can give a reading at your own church or for a group of friends or at a club you belong to. You will build confidence and then go on to groups that are less and less familiar to you. The dos and don'ts are just everyday common sense and courtesies you must remember to give to your audiences.

As for handouts, I never really found them to be effective and would often find a lot of them in the trash can at the end of the meetings.

As far as where I have gone and will go as an author, that is being driven with guidance from a power much greater than myself. Being a celebrity is not one motivated by my ego, but will be a tool to possibly help me reach even greater masses of people.

Steve Stevich is the author of *Stop Time and Reflect*

Overall Tips and Suggestions

♦

Slow and Steady Wins the Race
Hilde Lene Aardal

The emotional stress any author goes through while writing or publishing a book can be devastating. Therefore, as an author, I have a few simple rules I follow.

Multiply the amount of "time" you use by three and divide the amount of "work" you are going to do by three. It can take away a huge amount of stress and it diminishes the disappointment you feel if you "fail." Allowing time and less work as a factor can end up becoming a good resource.

I am used to giving speeches to a large number of people; not for my book, but in earlier days. I was never nervous. Why? I used an old trick I learned. I imagined everyone in front of me in clown outfits. When I did that, it made me smile and took the nervousness away.

"Write with your heart and edit with your brain"
Too many people have told themselves they can never write a book because they don't know how to "write correctly." I write with my heart. I allow thoughts to fly and my brain edits the work later.

"NO is never a failure"
If a publisher turns your work down, it only means they are looking for something else. It does not mean your work isn't good enough, and it's always possible to try somewhere else. Even if publishers do not accept your work, you have created something that is entirely your own.

Hilde Lene Aardal is the author of *The Mind's Eye*

Cause to Exist and Be Perpetuated

Jack Apostol

To innovate and create a market.

You have a gift of creativeness, but that should never be the end.

Your important thoughts must be made to radiate beyond the pages and not to be kept locked in between the covers of your book and in the solitude of seclusion.

In our books, we have a depository of ideas, and as people, are in a constant wave of mutual and reverberating echoes amongst each other's reactions to their individual interpretation to the sounds of variable thinking and actions; they should not vibrate diminutively to extinction and/or become silent and remain dormant and unassertive.

There must be an exchange of thoughts and ideas as an essential part of life, a reservoir and database of conceptions based on reason.

Why do writers, many times, suddenly falter and ignore their initiating force and discipline, the ingenuity, resourcefulness, and of their original arduous and distinctive nature of contriving to write a story, having it published, and then leave matters to chance?

Why is an author hesitant to partake in cooperation of co-actively marketing their works and encouraging the further support, augmenting and furthering the cause of their works to flourish?

It is a primary matter, a preeminent factor of their own important and personal nature and display of art, their own pride and forte of artistic value.

Man makes circumstances. Authors attain being published and then they leave the matter as it is.

Is it shyness or a lack of confidence, a lack of faith, or perhaps a fear to dare to be in a parallel conviction of themselves, or is it perhaps a lack of belief as a credence to a truth?

Nevertheless, they have overcome tremendous obstacles to become published, and now is not a point in time to vacillate and await the elusive infinite to work wonders on itself.

They have overcome significant means, endured duress, and projected great stamina, but their purpose is not really fully extrapolated to worldly minds.

In the matter of my own personal experience, upon completing my novel, *Not of Stones, But of Words*, I began immediately to write a play, *A Swim in the Stagnant Pool*. Then I ensued to write another novel *THE MONARCH OF HELL — A Diary After Death*, not being mindful initially of developing and promulgating "proper press" to facilitate its exposure to the outside world, assuming it to "happen itself."

At a moment of awakening, sort of "a day late and an adjective short," I suddenly proposed to lend a hand, and to promote and support PublishAmerica for their confidence and support on my behalf for having my works published.

Publishers need and expect input from their writers.

The fact arising is that we must be more assertive and aggressive on our own marketing strategies, rather than rely on fanaticism and mere imagination.

It can be wholeheartedly acknowledged, agreed, and common place for a writer, as it has been ceaselessly reiterated time and time again, for a writer to commit to exclaiming of the loneliness and frustrations of getting and committing to composition. Then, too, subsequently while writing, as to sustain a regular and persistent regimen of constructive thought and composition in the midst of an arena of conflicts between a subject and of its antagonizing confrontations amongst joys, happiness, and endeavors versus jealousies and hate.

The writer struggles stoically and diligently through the maze of emotions of contriving characterizations, plot, and of the arduous task of completing a story through their own distinctive and collective inventiveness and adaptability to create a cause.

Their motivating force compels the author to create, complete, and to fulfill their impressive and artful creation, but now however who is it that will publish their final skillful and proficient arrangement and flair of designed and unified accomplishment?

The aggregate sum of the whole against offering a book of literary work for publication is extraordinarily and incredibly high. It is in opposition to successfully having a publisher accept, reproduce, and having a book seen, portrayed, and represented in print, copyrighted, and available commercially in publishing houses and public libraries. Plays are especially more difficult as a marketable commodity to be accepted and have produced.

To actuate publicity for my novel and play, my local city of South Lyon/ Northville, Michigan, was notified factually of my first two published endeavors and they immediately gave me a front page pictorial write-up and review.

Secondly, I contacted The Library Network, a reciprocal borrowing/ lending library source encompassing over seventy-five separate metropolitan Detroit area city libraries in cooperation with one another, and provided them copies of my personal books for the initial purpose for their review. They were subsequently accepted and now my books are currently available to all of the separate and individual library units and of their subsidiaries within their given and expanded range throughout the area as mentioned.

Separately, the City of Detroit and the Dearborn Michigan Centennial Library also reviewed and accepted my books, that are currently in place upon their shelves.

Being of Greek heritage, announcements were made available to various Hellenic organizations of my documented literary credits, and then were later publicly printed as news of interest in the various monthly magazine bulletins issued by the various groups. Also, and in principal, this same information was treated individually and separately acknowledged as notices and printed by the various Greek Orthodox Churches in their regularly scheduled informative bulletins to their parishioners in our surrounding metropolitan area.

There are also high school and college alumni lists, or newsletters in essence, which could prove of benefit.

A pictorial and printed representative review of my published material was printed and inserted in the "Profiles" section of *THE METROPOLITAN GREEK CONNECTION*, a Greek-American Business Directory and Source Book (Great Lakes Area), and a functionary index of significant proportions.

The University of Michigan Library of Modern Greek Studies (Department of Classical Studies) also has my books on their shelf. Professor Vasilios Lambropoulos, of The University of Michigan, is a key advocate in that department. My books are also being submitted to The University of Michigan main campus library.

Therefore, positive ethnic associations with the individual does obviously present and can imply helpful suggestions for exposure and promotion.

At the moment, I am currently waiting for my new novel, *THE*

MONARCH OF HELL — A Diary After Death, to be published, and upon talking to the management of Barnes & Noble and of Borders, I have a tentative commitment and allotted time for a book signing appointment and session for all three of my works simultaneously. My works are on both of their lists, as well as on many other major bookstores and distributors throughout the United States online.

The Internet is a valuable source to conduct and research ways and lists for authors to contact and submit their written materials to editors and to agents specializing in various categorized subjects which are specific to multiple and variable services and subjects for the author in selling their writings.

A writer can also use a writer's list of literary agents found in most all reference sections of libraries, and are there for anyone seeking professional publishers and accredited agencies to represent and promote their literary achievements for the current adaptable and suitable market place.

As to having my play produced, *A Swim in the Stagnant Pool*, it is said that ninety-five percent of the plays produced have been sold, controlled, and managed by agents.

My next step is to find a suitable playwright agency or a screen writers' agency to perhaps make arrangements or negotiations for me to proceed in my search and quest for the ultimate goal of my own special hope of achievement relative to my play.

I am also preparing labels to contact members of The 70th Infantry Division Trailblazer Association. I have been nominated and have received The Outstanding Trailblazer Award from my Army peers, the highest award that they can present upon their own. My purpose is to announce my book *Not of Stones, But of Words*, facts therein pertaining to our factual World War II outstanding battlefield heroic and traumatic experiences.

Again, as to imply and bring to mind of my earlier ethnic issue and of me being a Greek/American "boy-soldier" as expounded in my war-oriented book, perhaps someone can perceive and take notice as to spark dual WW II enthusiasm in conjunction with a Greek ethnic box-office hit plot production for a movie and thereby to class it along with the successes of *My Big Fat Greek Wedding*, Nia Vardalos; *Zorba The Greek*, Anthony Quinn; *The Guns of Navarone*, Gregory Peck and Anthony Quinn; and *Never On Sunday*, Melina Mercouri? Wishful thinking or not, it's not impossible. Things happen!

There never seems enough time in life for a person to fulfill all of their hopes, desires, and anticipations. It is not fully understood and completely realized until a person has reached of age, and then its "back to the drawing board."

However, "Nothing ventured, nothing gained."

Jack Apostol is the author of *Not of Stones But of Words* and
A Swim in the Stagnant Pond

Who Does JK Think She Is?
Doug Arnold

Well, the answer to that is probably "a very hard-working writer."

Well, that may be the case, but JK Rowling has been extraordinarily successful at it. My question is: why?

Harry Potter is more than a successful book/film. I have no idea if bookstores have ever opened at midnight to serve a release before, but I would wager that neither they nor anyone else has ever had a massive crowd, in the middle of the night, nationally, as was in the UK. Reports of "hundreds, half way up the high street" were common.

Given that the written word is supposed to be dead, that seems not to correlate to me. Yes: The only market for academic books is academia. The only way to get your manuscript looked at is if the title contains the phrase: "Beckham" (UK); Madonna (US), or a four-letter double entendre. Most books, especially bios and auto bios, are never read. Then there are the big two Roman household gods: The Bible and Shakespeare, of course. So where do we start? Why bother? It's like spitting against the wind, surely?

Wrong.

If we look at different but similar phenomena, in other arts, we will see some very interesting parallels. Take music for example. If we take the beginning of contemporary music, one would have to say that its source was the same then as now: contemporary writers. Music has had its eighteenth-century geniuses. If we are making such a bold comparison, then Mozart must be Keats, or Shelley; Bach and Beethoven, Coleridge and Wordsworth. The rebels, Sebalius and Tchaikovsky, translate into William Blake. All of whom served the genteel classes.

With the advent of the Industrial Revolution came the new upper working class, artisans, foremen and shop floor managers, police officers, the list is endless. New disposable income brought along the music hall. Enlightened religious views allowed the music hall into church, and gospel was born.

From gospel, through jazz, big band, skiffle and rock and roll, we arrive at the phenomenon of the Beatles. From then on the new international megastar musician was created. Then came: The Kinks, The Stones, Donovan, Joan Baez, Dylan, The Who, Cream, Led Zeppelin, etc, etc, etc. Oh yes. And Sir Cliff Richard. He has had a hit record in the charts in every decade from the 1950s, and is still going strong.

In a similar vein, after The Romantics, like Mary Shelley, there were several big hits: Bram Stoker, Herman Melville, Charles Dickens, etc. Then there was Harry Potter. A new literary superstar has been created. The only thing that can follow is other megastar writers, just as other musicians followed on the waves of Beatlemania and still do today, so Harry Potter has created a worldwide wave of mania for books. And this rip curler has only just begun.

And what is the difference between JKR and other more run-of-the-mill good writers? She promotes her own books and marketing.

Now experience: I have at various times, been a fruiterer, florist, dug graves, built gardens, sold door to door, run my own firm, and been back to school. If experience has taught me nothing else, in my forty humble years, it is that President Truman's words are some of the wisest that have ever been spoken.

"There's no such thing as a free lunch."

The nearest person to me is next door. He does not know it yet, but he has bought a book.

Funnily enough, as far as I can see, there is no such thing as an objection to buying a book.

"I don't like your style of writing!"

I'm sorry. I'm just the author; you'll have to take that up with the publisher. That's $19.99, please.

"I can't read or write."

I'm sorry. I'm just the author; you can take that up with my publisher's audio department. That's $19.99, please.

"Your book is so bad that I am thinking of making a complaint to the environmental people about the waste of a good tree that could have gone on my barbeque."

I'm sorry to hear that. I am just the writer, of course. You need to contact publisher's environmental complaints department. That's $19.99, please.

So, for me, the most important thing is the customers that I find for myself. Now where is that list?

"One hundred people. I don't know one hundred people."

"Yes, you do."

The one set of people who are left off the list are the embarrassing ones. Don't be embarrassed. They do expect you to gift them a copy, because they are familyfriendsnextdoorsecondcousinstentimesremoved. Let Uncle Dave buy a copy. Would Uncle Dave drop his life and dedicate six-months hard labor, just to give you the results because you are his nephew/niece? No. So why should you? Put everyone on the list.

The best way that I have ever found of moving a product:

Yes, our books are not babies of our imagination, gently handed over to the nurses at PA; they are a product to flog. And there ain't no other way of selling anything, other than putting your face around and wearing out some shoe leather. I am even considering the possibility of actually canvassing door to door with copies in my carpet bag.

Suggestions from me will only reveal the same, as somebody else has said better. The message board is a superb source of material and fun too. The only thing that I can do is try what has worked for others. If that does not work, tune it a little to better fit you. If that does not work, try something else.

Some ideas that have crossed my mind have been discarded for one reason or another, mostly cost, but who needs to pay for publicity? I don't know about you, but I had some of those short stories that you either never tried to, or never got around to offering. I struck a deal with the editor of a free short-story site to look at my stories. If he likes them and posts them in his mag, he will pop an HTML in the blurb, to the sales site at PublishAmerica or Amazon, or whoever will take the sales. This method has three main advantages.

1. It costs nothing.

2. The people who read good short-story sites read new material for their recreational reading. It is a solid motherlode of potential readers. They are the stereotype who buys books. (Damn that grammar has a wooden leg: It's buy books and pooh to the verb contradiction.)

3. The third advantage is a result of the relationship I have with the readers: none. These are people whom I have never heard of and have no chance of seeing my book in their face, as a stand-alone book choice; yet, they are getting a sample of my style for free. If anyone buys one book, it is a bonus. Personally, I am very positive about it and suspect that I may be surprised by the possible results.

Other ideas I have gleaned, particularly by surfing the Internet a little, are:

Make yourself a graphic, perhaps the dust cover illustration. Watermark it into all your mail. Print it on your envelopes, you never know who handles your mail. Does your mail carrier curl up with a good read at the end of his/her shift? It doesn't take much lateral thinking to expand ideas like that. After all, if a bunch of novelists have no imagination, then we are all lost.

I am going to close, before I bore everyone to death, with a story:

The inventor Edison was visited by his doctor at the bequest of his family. They were sure he was going mad. When asked why he had wasted time on 657 experiments that did not work, the old man smiled. He looked up and said, "I know 657 ways not to make a light bulb." A few days later, he succeeded and the light bulb was invented. Edison was a few short of seven hundred attempts until he got it right.

Now whether that's urban myth or reality is irrelevant. The moral is the same whether it happened or not. The nineteenth-century British Prime Minister Disraeli, giving the shortest address to the Oxford University first-year students ever, stood up and said:

"Never give up. Never give up. Never ever give up" and sat down again.

Doug Arnold is the author of *Secret Tide*

Promotion Through Occupation
K.C. Borden, C.Ht.

Writing a non-fiction book relating to my clinical practice allows exposure to my work which I wouldn't have otherwise. Authors of published non-fiction work usually know their topic better than the prospective reader, or they wouldn't have been published. Half the battle is won when you know your information so well, you are a sought-after commodity.

Having been a clinical hypnotherapist for fifteen years, I have developed a widespread referral base. Clients come to see me for various reasons such as: depression, weight control, smoking, testing enhancement, athletic performance, and so on. I can see as many as fifteen new clients a week, as well as my mid-program participates. These individuals are exposed to my book each time they enter my office for counseling, and the majority will purchase the book, as it enhances the one-on-one program.

Most of the time, the clients will pass the book on to someone they feel can benefit from the self-help format, and buy another for personal use. Many times, a client will take orders, purchase several, and deliver them. This process feeds itself. Clients will buy the book, or someone who reads the book decides to become a client.

My clients are professionally diverse. One worked for a TV station and invited me to appear on a local "what's happening around the community" show to promote my book and clinic. I've been invited to hold several workshops regarding the program used in my practice. Other public events include participation with other authors in workshop settings, as guest speaker for clubs and organizations, in continuing education rosters, and as an informative speaker in university classrooms.

Another way my book is promoted, with no competition from other authors, is trade shows. As a hobby, my husband and I work a booth at gun-and-knife shows. I set up a nice display on one corner of the booth. Since it is unique to such shows, many stop and thumb through the book, read the back, look up at me, make the connection, and the interaction begins. Most of these people would be reluctant to go into a bookstore, and definitely wouldn't show up for a book signing. I sense these people find this encounter a rewarding experience, and often purchase the book, become a client, or both.

As you can see, self-promotion has been easy for me, but let's look at avenues available for most non-fiction writers.

Shyness is Out. You have to let others know what you do, and what you know. If you don't have the luxury of people seeking you out, seek them out. Civic organizations, many local PBS programs, churches, Chambers of Commerce, associations, and many other groups are constantly looking for someone to speak. Sending an announcement with short biography can put you on their list. Depending on your field of expertise, you may be able to register on your state roster to instruct for continuing education. Many disciplines require a number of hours each year to maintain a position in their field.

Most cities promote their local authors through an art fair. If so, this is an excellent place to promote yourself and your book.

Overcome Fear of Public Speaking. There is a technique, similar to biofeedback, I help my clients learn. Once established, this technique allows them to release negative emotions and regain positive control instantly.

For three days, sixty times a day, release the air in your lungs through you nostrils slowly and inconspicuously, each time a negative thought or action is in your environment. You can do this anywhere and at anytime, without anyone knowing what you are doing, or without it interfering with what you are doing. You don't have to think about, or direct this exercise. Example: If your ankle itches, you reach down and scratch it without thinking about what you're doing. In the same fashion, you don't have to analyze what you're doing, or why you're doing it. After three days, your body and mind will accept this practice, and you should regain positive control over your emotions. Then you can exhale slowly only when you want or need to breathe anything less than perfect away from you. If need be, you can go past the three days, to make sure your body and mind are reacting instantly to the slow breath.

This exercise is a valuable tool in my life. I have a heart defect, which allows my heart to run away, beating well over 200 beats a minute for up to two hours. I've learned to control my heart rate with this technique. When invited as a guest speaker, I use this exercise to keep the initial sixty-second adrenaline rush at bay. As I am being introduced, I exhale slowly, releasing all the air in my lungs. Calmness claims my emotions, and I totally avoid what was thought by many to be unavoidable: The sixty-second adrenaline rush. Where there is no fear, self-confidence resides.

K.C. Borden, C.Ht. is the author of *When Trying Fails, JUST DO IT*

Headed to Market

Jo-Brew

As soon as I had the art work for the cover of my book, I went to the printer. He made striking business cards, bookmarks, and letterhead that could be used as promotional flyers or stationery. My second step was to take the art work to my webmaster, who created an attractive webpage (*www.Jo-Brew.com*). I have since discovered several authors do their own bookmarks and postcards on the computer, but haven't found any as attention getting as mine.

I called local bookstores to find out who their author contact person was, called for an appointment, and then put together a folder to take with me. (Business cards, bookmarks, a letter presenting my book — *Preserving Cleo* — and clippings of newspaper announcements as I got them.)

I met with anyone who was willing to discuss a reading, then presented the book and left a copy for them to look at. Whenever possible, I left several books on consignment.

In the meantime, I asked for an author interview in our local newspaper and got it. I wrote a humorous essay and sent it to the same paper for the Write-In section. I wrote notes, talked about the book, and passed cards whenever I was in a group. I finagled announcements in the newsletters of four organizations I belong to. Out of those efforts, I got a reading at Barnes & Noble, two nearby independent book stores, three senior groups, a writing class at the community college, and a good-sized writing group. At the readings, I put up posters and had both bookmarks and business cards available. As time went by, I was invited to participate in three different art fairs, another opportunity to put my name out as well as present the book.

Every time I've done an appearance, I've tried to get at least one press release e-mailed to members of organizations I'm involved in, and do all I can to promote the event and sponsors.

During the summer, I attended the Pacific Northwest Writers' Conference in Seattle. One panel presentation I chose to attend was on marketing. Since the makeup of the panel included self-published authors, authors published in the standard way, and booksellers, I expected some new ideas. I wasn't disappointed.

After the marketing panel, I went back to the printer and ordered postcards with the striking cover art. (One of the presenters at the marketing panel pointed out that a postcard is seen by five people before it's delivered.) Next, I created a new address list, everyone I came in contact with, or ever had, was included. Each person on the list has received a postcard with an invitation to a reading or an announcement of an appearance.

The third major change was to find a gimmick — one that could be given to booksellers as an attention getter or a thank you. For me, it worked out to be a jar of local preserves which fit with both the theme and title of my book, *Preserving Cleo*. I also began serving the local preserves with snack crackers at readings whenever it was appropriate. All it took was two paper plates, preserves, crackers, and a plastic spoon.

I update my webpage regularly and have begun adding a seasonal essay to be read or downloaded for an extra smile. The last few readings I've put out a few pages from my new novel, not yet in print, and plan to put them on my webpage when I have a publication date.

As it gets closer to the time for the second book to come out, I've donated copies of the first to a few of the small libraries in our rural areas. I'm working on the theory that the more readers I have of the first novel, the more sales I'll have of the sequel.

These efforts haven't led to a bestseller list, but I keep making sales, meeting fellow authors who lead to new avenues, and finding enough encouragement to keep moving on.

Jo-Brew is the author of *Preserving Cleo* and *Cleo's Slow Dance*

My Experiences
H.Dietrich Brinkmeyer

I have tried to promote my first book in several categories. First was the local scene. Not much there really. My small town is just that. If everybody in town bought a book it still wouldn't make a dent. The local bookstores, if you can call them that, did not want to invest any money in an unknown author. I thought about how I could overcome this. I talked to two of them and asked them to take the book on consignment. The good side of this is they have to make no investment. I had to negotiate with the owners. The best I could do was a 60/40 split. I get the 60% if the book sold. They, of course, get the 40%. They have no risk. If the book doesn't sell, I come back and pick it up. They have nothing to lose. The trouble is I make no money on 60%. I agreed on some anyway just to get the publicity. It didn't work very well.

I tried to work on the "local writer makes good" theory. It didn't impress the bookstore managers the way I thought it would. I went to the local newspaper with that approach. They did print a rather long article about me and my book. Once when I was walking down the street a woman I didn't know stopped me and said, "You're the writer!" I didn't know her from Adam or Eve. However, that's the only response I'm aware of.

The second category was larger towns and larger bookstores. The first thing I encountered was the question — "What's the ISBN number?" They quickly punched it in the computer and said, "Sure, we can get that one for you anytime." But, they did not want to invest any money either. I asked how to get around this. They gave me the district manager's name and address. I called or wrote, but not much action there either. I did this for several stores. So, I tried a different approach. I made up a packet of the book, with my name and address, a SASE, a cover letter describing the book and a request to reply and return my book. Sometimes I got neither. I asked if I could set up a book signing booth or whatever and sign books in their store. The reply in one was – "Go ahead, but you better bring something to read yourself because you

112

won't be very busy." They were right. I had four such sessions, but didn't net many books. Both the large and small bookstores told me they had arrangements with wholesale book suppliers.

I realize I'm not giving you the positive feedback you are seeking, but maybe some good can come from what didn't happen. I tried to analyze "why." Although I know you have heard it many times, I think it is true – you have to know someone. I do think that's the answer. I read in *Time* about a year ago or more about the book *The Prayer of Jabez*. It was a best seller — in its category. I also read that it was published by a "small publisher" in Sisters, Oregon. I know Sisters; it is a small town. This encouraged me to proceed. If Bruce Wilkinson can do it, so can I. I found out later that he was a well-known speaker around the nation and associated with the Dodson Ministries. I didn't know that, should have guessed. This reinforced the "got to know someone" theory. I didn't know exactly what to do about this.

I thought about jumping off a bridge and when they rescued me I could say, "Buy my book!" Haven't done that yet. I did decide to try *some* approach. I decided to invest the cost of some books — a few anyway — so I picked out some well-known organizations that I thought fit my book style. The first was the Billy Graham Ministries. I sent a complimentary copy with a flowery cover letter to Mr. Billy Graham himself.

I realize he is not into promoting books, other than his own, but I just wanted to get it in the hands of a well-known and respected person. Who knows what will happen after that. I did get a very nice letter, I thought from Mr. Graham thanking me for the book, etc. Nothing more so far. I decided not to ask for the books back when I did this because I wanted them to be around in their environment so they could be seen — I hope. I can't afford to give too many away.

I have also contacted book clubs, etc. requesting a review of my book. Some agreed to receiving the book but reminded me that they receive "millions"!? Also, they didn't agree to return the book.

I hope this sad story has some good sides — maybe what not to do. I certainly do agree that we authors need some assistance and guidance in promotion.

H.Dietrich Brinkmeyer is the author of *'Bout Them Angels* and *Mississippi Mud*

The Ladder to Success

Annettee Budzban

It has been said that some people spend their lives climbing the ladder to success only to find it leaning against the wrong building. As a published author, where are you leaning your ladder?

As soon as my book, *Life Changing Inspirations*, was published, I quickly realized its success was up to me. Promoting my book brought with it an extra challenge, as I was housebound with an illness. However, I started to pray and read about the different ways I could promote my book.

Since I write short stories and devotions, I started to look for places that would publish my type of writings and give me a byline. (This is a spot at the end of your article about three or four lines long, where you can give a short author bio, and plug your book.) I soon came across many Internet sites that publish my type of writings and started submitting. Before long, I found myself published on many of them. This is also a great way for worldwide recognition.

My next idea came when I noticed some writers of my genre wrote newspaper columns. I started calling newspaper editors in the area and informing them I was a published author interested in submitting some samples of my writing for a column proposal. I now write weekly columns for two newspapers. I am pursuing more.

I still seek and search for new ideas and publications to make myself known. I strive to stay realistic that few of us are shooting stars. Most of us become successful by the law of progress — "little by little." With this thought in mind, I will not become discouraged when I am not an overnight success. (Don't misunderstand, I never underestimate this possibility either.) Instead, it daily gives me the drive to continue my quest for success!

Annettee Budzban is the author of *Life Changing Inspirations*

Promoting a Published Author
Joseph-Jony Charles

Get this into your head first: As a published author, you only have one book to promote. It's up to you to get it done. You can do a much better job than the publishers, who have hundreds and thousands of authors' works to promote. Yes, you can always benefit from their marketing powers, but they have limited ad budgets. We all wish they could send us on book tours. That's not always the reality of book publishing for many of us, debutante authors. Turn your friends and acquaintances into peer-to-peer marketers. Word of mouth will champion your book.

Once I knew that my book, *The Long Lost Garden of Eden*, was going to be published, I started making plans on how I would place it in the hands of readers. I was ready to get behind the book 100%. All published authors should realize that they are the best persons to push the book. For one thing, the public enjoys interacting with an author who presents his/her book. Even when a copy is not sold as a result of an interaction, the word of mouth gets started. Published authors need to have a plan to be able to build this groundswell of support from the various local entities such as former teachers, church, local colleges and universities, high schools, middle schools, local book clubs, senior-citizen villages, barbershops, gym or fitness centers, or any other businesses that are related to your book.

What I have found to be useful is the creation and maintenance of two websites: *http://bookstore.shopnowshop.com* and *http://www.geocities.com/longlostgardenofeden*. Your readers can get more info about your books and other writings.

As long as the author can afford it, he/she should try to buy copies of the book. It's a good way to show your interest in your own book. At the same time, you can use these copies for special autographed requests or sales.

Published authors should never rest on their laurels. They should be actively involved in sending out press kits and letters to writing programs, teachers as mentioned above, influential people in their community, librarians and local media people. Never hesitate to conduct a reading and workshop when you have the opportunity to do so. It's worth noting that the press kits can contain good or bad articles. Obviously, more emphasis may be placed on the good ones.

What I have found out is that some people may want to know what's in it for them. If they are hosting some book reading event for you, they will benefit from the association and publicity that your book creates. In my experience with hosts, I'd advise you to be nice and generous to them. They'll do so much for you if you treat them with respect. After all, they can contribute to your success. Never hesitate to take advantage of a reading, signing, and workshop. These avenues will help you get and stay connected.

Just know that if you don't promote it, you'll have a dead book. You must do whatever it takes to bring attention to it. If the buying public does not know about it, they won't purchase it, no matter how good it may be.

A few more tips that should be part of your plan right off the bat:

* Identify your niche markets and approach them. Talk to your publisher's marketing department. They don't always know the resources in your community.

* Contact other published authors from your community. They may offer some advice to you. They have developed some tricks. You can always contact them. All they can do is to say no.

* Remember that when one door gets closed, many others open up.

Good luck selling your book!

Joseph-Jony Charles is the author of *The Long Lost Garden of Eden*

Lessons in Marketing My Book
Joan Clayton

What was the first thing I had to overcome in marketing my first book? ME! It's hard to promote myself. I felt "tooting my own horn" brought out a giant-sized ego. What would people think of me, I wondered. I am a Christian writer and I characterized that what I had to say might have a hint of pride. With God's help, I overcame that feeling. He put the message in my heart to share, so who am I to doubt it? The world needs to know there is a better way to live.

With that in my heart, I boldly started marketing my first book. Testing the waters, I took several free copies to the gift shop in our local hospital. This led to several orders, as patients began to feel like reading.

Next, I asked my dentist if he minded if I left a copy in his waiting room. His hygienist told me later that when she called a patient's name he or she didn't want to put the book down, and wanted to know where to get a copy. In fact, while in the waiting room one visit, another patient picked up the book and asked me if I knew the lady who wrote it. What a thrill!

We have several boutique stores in our area and they bought several copies of my first book. They displayed them in a most decorative way. One store surrounded my book with pearls and roses. It made me want to buy my own book!

Managers of bookstores (Christian or not) gladly received a few free copies to "prime the pump." They displayed them on the counters by the cash registers and customers browsed through the pages while waiting for change.

On my new book, I plan to invest some money in posters. A local print shop charges a minimum fee for just ten posters. "Each Day is a Gift by Joan Clayton" (with a small photo) will be featured on the poster. Smaller printed words will have some excerpts from my book: "A daily devotional guide to strengthen families. Strong families build strong nations." I will ask bookstores if I might display the poster. If they do not agree, I will leave a free copy of my new book anyway. Someone will buy it and want more for gifts.

I will leave a free copy at the large church I attend. They will put it in the church library. I also plan to buy an ad in a church periodical. I have been a regular contributor to a little devotional magazine for many years, so my name is out there already.

We have several radio stations in my area. First, I will dress up and make a friendly impression. I will make an appointment to meet the new manager, leading to interviews. Previously, I was invited to give short, verbal, Easter messages on the air, which gave me credibility.

With my new book, I plan to write several bookstores in larger cities, telling them why I wrote the book and why people need my book. In the aftermath of 9/11, we need a blueprint for recovery.

I will order several copies of my book. I will send them to friends and relatives who live far away. I did this with my first book and what a reaction! In the course of six months, one lady bought 12 books to give as Christmas gifts. A man in another town bought 25 to give to business friends. To my surprise, my book went into second printing, and that was just my first book!

Bookstores have graciously offered book signings, and I joyfully accept, but don't be too disappointed if not many are sold that way. However, it's a good idea to make friends with bookstore employees, especially the managers. It's one point of contact.

Another contact is your local newspaper. Many will print your photo with a short write-up just to have the news. If not, most papers will print in the "briefs" a short statement of your name, the title of your book and where it can be obtained.

It takes leg work to get your message out and the world needs to hear it. After all, you are selling yourself and what you have to say. You have spent long tedious hours, days and months "birthing this baby." You believe in it. You know it's good. Be enthusiastic. Be positive.

You're a winner!

Joan Clayton is the author of *Each Day is a Gift*

Getting the Word Out About Your Words!

J. Paul Cooper

One of the most important principles in sales is establishing a rapport with the customer. That's the reason that an insurance agent will see the golf clubs in your basement and talk about golf for fifteen minutes before insurance is even mentioned. As you read these lines, you may have several thousand potential customers for your book, and you already have something in common with them. It will only cost you the price of a stamp or the time it takes to send an e-mail to let them know about your book.

Whether you've attended high school, university, military college, or a seminary, chances are they have an alumni association. A quick search of the school's website should provide you with a link to the school's alumni organization. Schools love to print announcements about their former students' achievements and having a book published is a significant achievement. One announcement on the website or alumni magazine has the potential to reach thousands of former students around the globe.

Another inexpensive method for reaching potential customers for your book is by writing personal essays about your book. Does your book have an interesting history? How long did it take to write the book? Was writing the manuscript an emotionally trying experience? What did you learn about yourself while you were writing the book? Has writing the book helped you learn anything new about the craft of writing? What inspired you to write the book?

The next time you visit the library, take some time to ask a librarian which publications on the magazine rack include personal essays. Then do an online search with "personal essay" as your subject and find out which websites publish personal essays. Although it's always great to receive a check in the mail for your writing, you may not be offered any payment for your personal essay. What's more important is how many people read the magazine or visit the website.

A personal essay presents you with an opportunity to generate interest in your book and also allows you to introduce yourself to readers. A one- or two-paragraph description on a book cover will not reveal as much about your personality as a personal essay.

One of the best ways to promote your book, and build your self-confidence as an artist, is to read at open mics whenever you have the opportunity. Reading from your book at an open mic at a local library or book club will help you prepare for the time you do a reading at a bookstore or literary festival and you're the main attraction. Reading in front of an audience allows you to develop a good pace. That's important, because if you read too fast, the audience won't understand you, and if you read too slowly, they'll find you boring.

If you take a walk through a shopping mall it's easy to spot who the sports fans are, because they'll be wearing the jerseys of their favorite teams. It is, however, very unlikely that you'll find a group of writers sitting around the central fountain, typing on their laptop computers. If you want to get to know other people who share a passion for words, visit your local libraries and bookstores and ask if they know about any writers' groups that meet in your area. Other writers will be able to give you advice on promoting your book, and there's no better way to meet new friends and fire up your passion for writing, even during the worst case of writer's block.

J. Paul Cooper is the author of *Fluffy: A Cat's Tale*

The Simple Steps of Promoting Your Book

Annette DeLore

I am not going to beat around the bush; your book is published at this point, so what's ahead of you now? Tons of work...and I do mean WORK. You have just entered the world of becoming a salesperson. It is truly up to you, not your publisher, to make your book either fly the skies or hit the rock pile. With that said, let's get to work on promoting your book.

First, we need to set you up with a few tools to get you started. These tools will become one of your best friends and will help you out more than I can express! I am listing them in the order that I would recommend for you to follow.

1. Get on the Internet and set up a free website. More than one is even better, but, hey, starting with one is good. (Notice I said "free"?) So now you're asking, where do I find free websites? Here's a few to get you going: *www.authorsden.com*, *www.geocities.com* and *www.freeservers.com*.

2. Set up an e-mail address for business only, maybe at one of your websites or through Hotmail. The choice is yours.

3. Snail-mail address. This can either be at your home address or a P.O. Box. Again, the choice is yours.

Now that we have your website, e-mail, and snail mail set up, the next step should be very easy for you.

4. Business cards (which I refer to as website cards and I'll explain that later) and bookmarks. The information you want on these cards is listed in

steps 1-3; you should also include the name of your book. If you choose to put your phone number on these as well you may; however, do you really want everyone you give a card to calling you? So what I do is have two sets of cards printed and put my phone number on only one set. This set is for bookstores, agents, and so on. Don't know where to get business cards and bookmarks done? Here are a few ideas: Any quick print shop, office supply store, or the cheapest I've found are at *www.vistaprint.com.*

Now that we have our business/website cards done, we are ready for the next step in promoting your book. Take a deep breath — this is where the fun/ work really begins. The time has come to start making your contacts, and introducing yourself to the public as a published author. For some of you, this may seem to be the hard part. You're wondering to yourself, "How in the world do I do that?" Easy, but always remember to bring a copy of your book, and your business/website cards.

5. Contact your local library and any libraries in nearby towns. Tell them that you'd enjoy doing a book reading for them. You'll be pleasantly surprised how many libraries will be thrilled to have you there. Also, become a member of the "Friends of the Library"; this will gain you tons of great information.

6. At this point, you've landed yourself a "public appearance" at one or more libraries. This is "news" to your area! Call or walk into your local radio stations, and the ones in nearby towns. (Remember — book and business/ website cards in hand when you walk in.) Tell them about your "book reading" dates and times at the library. This will spark their interest in you, and you now have landed a live radio interview. Be sure to ask the DJ, who is going to interview you, if you may have a tape of the interview. Most radio stations will be more than happy to give you one.

7. TV stations. If you have a local one, by all means, stop in and visit them! Apply the same thing at the TV station as you did at the radio station. This could land you an interview on the station's news program. After all, you are a local celebrity, and your book is news!

8. Next, contact your local newspaper. Be sure NOT to contact the newspaper of whatever town you're doing your reading in until after your radio and TV interviews. Most radio and TV stations will balk if you go to the newspapers first. Radio stations DON'T want to be second in reporting news,

and TV stations don't mind if you were on the radio first.

Tell the newspaper about your book reading at the libraries and about your book. This will be sure to get you an interview in the newspaper, not to mention free publicity for your appearance at the library. Also, it's okay to mention to the newspaper that the local radio and TV stations have interviewed you. This will make you more of a celebrity to them and chances are you will end up on the front page.

At this point, you should be seeing how easy this is. You are now on your way to building your "media kit." What's a media kit, you ask? This is the next step of promoting yourself as an author to bookstores for a book signing.

9. Media kit. This is one of the most important tools that an author can have. You'll be adding to your media kit as time goes on. Remember the newspaper interviews that you cut out from the newspapers? Make a few copies of them and always be sure to keep the original in a safe place. Get yourself a folder and place a copy of your interviews and business/website card in the folder. This is what you take to the bookstore with you and give to the bookstore manager as you promote yourself for a book signing with their store. This shows the bookstore manager that having a book signing with you could be very worthwhile.

10. Now, remember that website of yours? You have posted the fact that you are having a reading at the library, not to mention that you've also been interviewed by radio, TV and the newspapers, haven't you? Whenever you are going to appear anywhere, ALWAYS post it on your website.

11. Have you thought about getting your book reviewed? If not, get on the Internet and look up book reviewers. Write them a letter or e-mail and ask them about doing a book review of your book. (Hint: This is another good thing to put in that media kit you are building, not to mention on your website.)

12. Celebrities are good people to contact. There are several of them that have been more than willing to read a first-time author's book and do a review. (Hint: When you get a review from a celebrity, be sure to put it in your media kit.) A good place to find out how to contact a celebrity is at your local library in the Who's Who Book.

13. So, do you think your book would make a great movie? Don't be afraid to contact the movie production companies. Get on the Internet, and do your homework on who to contact.

14. Finding an agent. My best advice on finding an agent is in the book called, *Guide to Literary Agents*. This is published by Writers' Digest Books. You may visit their website at: *www.writersdigest.com*. WARNING! BEWARE of the SHARKS! A shark is any agent who charges a fee to do a "reading" of your book or manuscript. Any agent who wants to charge you a "monthly service," STAY AWAY FROM! An honest agent will be paid by a percentage of the sales of your book. Most agents charge 12 to 15 percent.

As I mentioned in step four, the reason I refer to my business cards as website cards is that the reaction from the public, store managers, etc. is so much more positive. Business cards have a tendency to sound like you're a salesperson, only wanting to sell your product (which we really do); however, offering your website card is not a pushy sales pitch, and, first and foremost, we are authors trying to build a reader following.

Sending someone to your website to learn about you, the author, and your book(s) will draw more interest in you. After all, how many business cards have you been handed in the past, and you just threw them away? A website card is not a sales pitch; it's an invitation that says, "Visit my site, get to know me."

These are only the basic steps in getting you started on promoting your book. In closing, I wish you well, and remember to enjoy the promoting process of your book. Please feel free to e-mail me, or visit my websites and leave a message.

Annette DeLore is the author of *Prisoner of the Heart*

Promotions

Sharon Ervin

When I contacted Steve, the dean of independent booksellers, about my forthcoming first book, he insisted I bring the book and come talk to him in person before he would agree to allow a signing at his store. The day came.

Scowling, he examined the book for workmanship, print, quality of paper, etc., before he pronounced, "This is a very nice book," and "Yes, we'll do a signing here."

He told me to have cards and bookmarks and posters made and emphasized, "Put your picture on everything." He insisted the result would justify the expense.

I hate pictures of me, but I did have a new one, made for the book cover. He waved my objections aside and said, "Author recognition is important. Do it anyway."

Layout is not my forte, so I went to a local print shop and told them basically what I needed. They produced enchanting, spectacular proofs and I told them so, repeatedly. We all appreciate being appreciated. They repaired a couple of typos and I ordered two-hundred-fifty cards (the smallest quantity they printed), five hundred bookmarks and thirty flyers.

An old newspaper reporter, I contacted every paper I had worked for, and the newspapers and some radio stations of every town where I had ever lived or worked. Editors had moved on but, because of the connection, current staff agreed to give me some ink if I would send a book and/or a press kit.

Press kit — I put one together, enclosing a card, a bookmark, a flyer, a brief bio and picture, a blurb about the book and even a picture of the book's cover. When they requested it, I also enclosed a book — a freebee. That was expensive, but may be worthwhile.

Most organizations — charitable, service, civic, women's groups — have newsletters and magazines. I contacted every one of those with whom I had even a remote affiliation. My college sorority, university, church, and clubs all had magazines and all were receptive.

I had guest lists from three weddings and gleaned names from those. From high school reunions, I got rosters of old classmates (I attended two high schools). The publisher offered to send announcements if I would provide the address labels. I did and was astonished to come up with seven hundred names. And I e-mailed friends, family, casual acquaintances, and groups.

Then, taking courage in hand, I went into a Barnes & Noble store in Dallas where no one would know me and I might never show my face again, if things went badly. I waited in line for a clerk, then lowered my voice to say I had written a book and I wondered about doing a book signing in their store.

The young male clerk alerted everyone within thirty feet. "We have an author here. Here's an author. Right here."

I was mortified. "No, no. This is not an important book. It's just a paperback. I'm not famous or an expert or anything."

Two assistant managers and several clerks surrounded me and examined the book. Yes, they would set up a book signing. They checked their computers. If they couldn't get the books, would I bring some? They acted like my book and I were honored guests. Gee. One manager eventually said, "Authors create the product we sell. We make our living off what you do."

Wow.

I was bolder from then on, approaching managers at big chains, small independent stores, Hallmark stores, Wal-Marts, drug and grocery stores and libraries. I have never actually gotten over being amazed at their kind attention.

Steve had said smile at everyone and do not complain. He had been right so far, so I did as he said. Sometimes, at a book signing, smiling is an effort. Sometimes you just have fun.

I am a woman of intimidating size and discovered that I sell more books if I remain seated in one spot rather than roaming. I make eye contact with people, smile, speak and offer them a bookmark. Some people are on a mission and don't want the distraction. Some, at first, don't realize I am selling my own book and are genuinely amazed that the picture on the cover is me.

To men, I suggest my books as gifts for wives, girlfriends, sisters, coworkers. To women, I suggest my books might put a little steam in their lives.

One beautiful Saturday in Tulsa, the weatherman had predicted the 70-degree temperature would drop rapidly and possibly snow that night. I told several ladies that when they were snowed in on Sunday, they were going to wish they had bought a copy of my book. Two or three did. Five returned to the store the next day, in the snow, to buy signed copies I had left behind. Although I was not present, they laughingly mentioned my warning.

Every organization has program chairpersons who are desperate for speakers of any ilk. When they ask, I say yes. I have spoken to groups from ten members to 250. I tell them a few highlights of my experiences with writing, entertain comments from the floor and give plenty of time to questions and answers. Closet writers are everywhere, keeping diaries, journaling, documenting trips or family memories. I tout writing as an excellent way to vent — grief, joy, anger — every emotion that is part of the human condition.

Promoting my books is not just good for sales, I pick up new dialogue, fresh thoughts, see a vast array of body types, facial expressions, fashions, all of which feed the creative juices which produce another book to be accepted by a publisher who will require an updated bio and picture, new cards and bookmarks and more book signings and speeches.

I love writing, though it is solitary work. I also like people. Promotion is people kind of work. Whichever I am doing, Steve's advice holds true. Produce a book you can be proud of, then be proud of it.

And smile.

Sharon Ervin is the author of *Jusu and Mother Earth* and *Bodacious*

Using Poetry to Promote
John Gorby

I have been writing Christian poetry for almost five years. About two years ago, I started putting them in frames, and selling them at work. After I finished writing my book, *Plant a Seed*, I read that you should start trying to promote your book long before it's available in stores. So far, I have my framed poems in three different stores; a gas station, a garden store, and a restaurant. I went to my local paper and got permission to write a press release about my poetry. They are going to mention the three stores my poems are being sold at! The people at the businesses liked the idea of free advertising. They have all said, when my book comes out, they want to carry it, too!

I also went to a Christian radio station's remote broadcast, and met the station manager. I gave him one of my framed poems about a lighthouse. I told him that when my book comes out, I will get back with him; he said that would be good.

Anything you can think of, try it! I also carry them with me in my trunk. Wherever you stop, strike up a conversation, and end up talking about your writing! Most people I have talked to enjoy hearing about something that's uplifting, that someone has had a dream come true.

Now when I mention I write poetry, and show them some of my poems, I often hear, "I've seen some of your poems!" You are going to be your best promotional tool. Go out and make yourself visible, and hand out business cards, letting them know they can have access to you! This is a special opportunity, make the most of it.

John Gorby is the author of *Plant A Seed*

Get Ready

Dan Graffeo

If you're reading this, you're either a) a family member or friend that is supporting me or b) a writer who is determined to market his or her book to its full potential. If it is the former, thank you for your time. If it is the latter, let me tell you what I have learned.

The best advice I can give you in promoting your book is to get ready. Get ready to spend money, get ready for yet more rejection in your struggle for success, and get ready for a job outside your job. When my novel, *Blood Drops on Roses*, came out, I was working in a hotel from six a.m. to two p.m. When I punched out, I began the other shift. For at least six hours a day, I took immediate action to market my book to the public. I mailed flyers to every bookstore between Worcester and Nantucket. I called every newspaper in my area. I e-mailed every local radio station. I spent hundreds of dollars printing up full-color bookmarks that had information about my book written on them. I passed these bookmarks out everywhere I went: horror conventions, movie theater break rooms, restaurants, hotels, music stores, comic book stores, supermarkets, and, of course, local bookstores.

Unfortunately, despite my constant efforts, 95% of all the businesses and media outlets I mentioned above denied helping me in any way. Radio stations want sizeable fees to mention any product over the air. Most local newspapers never got back to me and some shunned the idea of mentioning a horror novel in their respected and sophisticated pages. Of the dozens of local bookstore managers I spoke with, only four agreed to shelf my novel, and that was only if I supplied the copies for them. As frustrating as that was, bear in mind that this is also understandable. Most bookstores don't want to take a chance with an author unless that author is famous. This is a business, and a tough one at that. You must be creative in promoting your book.

My creative promotion was having a commercial made. I wrote out a 30-second script that gave the reader (or viewer) a pitch of what my book was about, and then had a film student friend of mine help me promote it like a movie. It aired twice a day on FX and the Sci-Fi channel during Halloween week. This kind of advertising can be expensive, but the old saying is true: You have to spend money to make money.

Promoting your book can be fun, if you let it. Remember, your book is a symbol of who you are, regardless of genre or subject. Being published means that you have an obligation to share it with the world, and not just for profit. Your book should enrich your life, and the lives of the lucky ones who get to peek at your inner soul.

Allow me to wish you the best of luck.

Dan Graffeo is the author of *Blood Drops on Roses*

Hints from the
Director of a PR Firm
Alvin Guthertz

First, allow me to establish my background:

* Two PublishAmerica books are now out — *Low Fog in Eden* and *Namanga*. My third book, *Magnets for Love*, is also being published by PublishAmerica.

* I have directed my own San Francisco-based PR firm for over 35 years.

* Have won numerous writing awards and contests.

* My writing has gotten me all over the world, including to a Royal wedding (Fergie and Prince Andrew); Trooping the Colors (with the Queen on the balcony directly behind me); into Scotland Yard's Black Museum (not open to the public); to the Academy Awards; even to a nude beach in Tahiti.

* Authors I've represented include: Margaret Truman, Belva Plain, Rhona Jaffe, and the late James Clavell.

A Few Brief PR and Marketing Suggestions:

* Prior to the official release of your book, start "leaking" to local newspaper columnists and radio DJs. (*The New York Times* likes a copy four months in advance.)

* Send copies of your book to local book editors. Prepare a *proper* press release. This might include information about the book, the author's background, or perhaps a photo.

* Makes sure you know how to write a press release — who, what, when, where in the first paragraph. Be sure to include contact information. Have a *brief* cover letter spelling out all personal information (i.e. how to contact the author, in case they may have any questions.) It's okay to call or e-mail the editor *once* to let them know it's coming. DON'T BE A PEST — they work on strict deadlines.

* Arrange local TV and radio interviews. Again, have a press kit sent in advance along with the cover letter.

*Contact local bookstores, letting them know about the book, and the local PR it will receive. Tell them you can mention their names during interviews.

* During the interview, when answering questions, say the title of your book. DON'T just say "the book" or "my book," etc.

* Stay aware of breaking news stories which might relate to your book — this can give an added followup to the media.

* Arrange talks for local groups.

Alvin Guthertz is the author of *Low Fog in Eden, Namanga,* and *Magnets for Love*

10 Basic Secrets of
Book Publicity for Authors
Denny Hatch

My first job after the Army in 1960 was in the publicity department of Prentice-Hall's trade-book division, writing press releases and getting authors on radio and television. In the ten months I was there, I learned to take the galley proofs of a full-length book, know what was in it and have a finished two-page press release written, all in the space of two hours. The highest compliment I could receive was when a book critic signed my release and called it his review. This happened more than once. What is different today and what can you do about it?

1. Nine Words of Advice for Authors Regarding Book Publicity
Expect to spend money. Expect little from your publisher.

2. What to Expect from the Publisher's Publicity Department
When I was at Prentice-Hall in 1960, we provided good publicity and promotion. According to the World Almanac, a total of 15,012 titles were published that year and we would spend time planning and executing effective publicity and promotion. Today, with more than 60,000 titles published every year, reviewers and publicity departments are stretched piano-wire tight. Unless you are the author of raging best sellers, your title might rate half a day's work on the part of one very junior in-house publicity person, who will not have read your book. Your attitude: You spent a ton of time creating the book, spend a ton more promoting it. And some money.

Here are the bare-bones basics of what needs to be done:

(a) Jacket copy written;

(b) Press release written;

(c) Review slip created. This is a small, single sheet with all the info about your book: title; author; number of pages; binding; ISBN number; publication date; publisher's name, address, phone, E-mail, and fax number; where to mail, fax or e-mail a copy of the review.

(d) All of the above, plus a personal letter, should be sent with a bound galley to the early review media three to four months in advance of publication date. Those media (about 15 organizations) include PW, Lj, ALA Booklist, Choice, etc.

(e) When finished books arrive in the warehouse, labels and personal letters should be created and sent with the release and the review slip to the major book review media (my "A" list contains 55 names). If the book is a specialty title (e.g., cookbook, business book, computer book, gardening book, children's book, etc.), the publisher should have a list of reviewers in those specific areas and should send review copies to them. Make sure the publicity department is doing this. If it is not, jump in and help out.

3. Specialty Reviews
My first mentor in the business, children's publisher Franklin Watts, used to say he would send a review copy to anyone that could generate the sale of 5 or more copies. Who do you know who can do that — reviewers, bookstore owners, specialty-shop owners, online services? Make a list and either get your publisher to send review copies or do it yourself. Remember to send the press release with the review copy, this tells about the book and about you. Give it a news slant. Personalize the letter, talking directly to the reviewer about the benefits of the book to that reviewer's specific audience.

4. Hire a Freelance Publicist
If you are uncomfortable blowing your own horn, hire a *well-connected* freelancer. They come at all prices and varied experience. How much to pay? Figure on $1,000 to $50,000. Let the publisher know you are doing this and make sure review copies will be made available. You are hiring a Rolodex as well as a publicist. Who do you hire? Ask to talk to other authors this person has represented. A good freelance publicist can get you bookings to do talks and appear on radio and television.

5. Make Nice with Booksellers and Librarians
Offer to do a talk and a book signing at every bookstore you can identify and get to. Same thing for libraries.

6. Have Books

If you do get a bookstore or library gig, make sure the publisher has books there for you to sign — and not the day after, but the day of.

7. Don't Start with Publicity Until Books Are in the Warehouse

Too many eager authors want to get the word out. The word gets out and people want to buy and with no books available, you have lost the sale. (Exception: The early reviewers mentioned in #2 above.)

8. Alert Everyone You Ever Met in Your Life

Send a note or a postcard to everyone you ever met in your life, from kindergarten to the people in your current company.

9. Prowl the Internet

Get word of your book on every relevant website you can find. Make absolutely sure the information about your book at Amazon.com and Barnesandnoble.com is correct.

10. Get Free E-mail Newsletters on Book Publishing, Publicity, and Promotion

A number of very savvy book promoters are out there on the Internet who can help turn you into a pro. Three of the best are: Dan Poynter (*http://www.parapublishing.com*); John Kremer (*http://www.bookmarket.com*); Brian Jud (*http://www.bookmarketingworks.com*). Sign up for their free newsletters on book publicity and promotion. If they come to town with their traveling seminar on book promotion, by all means attend. I did and learned a lot.

Denny Hatch is the author of *PRICELINE.COM:*
A Layman's Guide to Manipulating the Media.
He is a direct marketing consultant and
contributing editor of *Target Marketing* magazine.

How I Promoted My Book
Lillian B. Herzberg

The Internet was a great help in finding addresses of groups to which I belonged. I wrote either to e-mail addresses or snail mail to the people in charge of programming. I included a brief bio, a short summary of my book and a letter telling the group why they would be interested in hearing about it. I also was willing to make a small contribution to the organization. I feel I was very successful. I intend to do the same thing with my second book, *Stephan's Journey - A Sojourn Into Freedom*, soon to be published by PublishAmerica.

Lillian B. Herzberg is the author of *Kindness of Strangers* and
Stephan's Journey - A Sojourn Into Freedom

15 Commandments for Getting FREE Publicity

Carolyn Howard-Johnson

A huge retailer once said that advertising works, we just don't know how, why, or where it works best.

What we do know is that advertising's less-mysterious cousin, publicity, works even better. It is the more reliable relative because it is judged on its merit alone and carries the caché of an editor's approval. It also is surrounded by the ever-magic word "free." The two are easily identified as kin.

These two often walk hand in hand and yet they can be incompatible. The editors of good media outlets will not allow the advertising department to influence them. Still, in an effort to be completely impartial, they reserve the right to use advertiser's stories editorially if they deem them newsworthy. That is why it is helpful to use advertising in a vehicle that plays to the audience you would like to see standing in line for your book. This paid-for exposure then becomes an entrée to the decision-makers. A contact in the advertising department may be willing to put a news release on the desk of one of his editors, maybe even encourage her to look at it. There are no contracts, but it does sometimes work. If you're going to try this route, choose a "little pond" — a bookish brochure or an "arty" weekly — so that the dollars you spend will be noticed.

Sometimes a magazine or newspaper will run a special promotion called an advertorial. These are sections where you pay for an ad and then the newspaper assigns a reporter to cover the story you want told. The article carries some of the prestige of editorial copy — that is, the general reader may assume the article has been chosen only on its merits because of its copycat character. The writer or editor you meet can be approached when you have something exceptional.

Fellow author Erin Shachory (Eshachory@aol.com), who handles consumer publicity and consults on advertising strategies, knows that her clients hire her—at least in part—for her "great database." It is something that, over time, you can build for yourself.

Still, an advertorial isn't exactly FREE. If FREE sounds more like the fare that will serve your needs, carve out some time to do it yourself and follow these 15 commandments for doing it:

Educate yourself: Study other press releases. Read a book like *Publicity Advice & How-To Handbook*, by UCLA Marketing Instructor, Rolf Gompertz, a SPAN member. Join publicity-oriented e-groups.

Read, read, read: Your newspaper. Your e-zines. Even your junk mail, a wonderful newsletter put out by the Small Publishers of North America (*www.spannet.org*) and one called The Publicity Hound (*www.publicityhound.com*). My daughter found a flyer from the local library in the Sunday paper stuffed between grocery coupons. It mentioned a display done by a local merchant in the library window. Now we're going to have one for my book, too. Rubbish can be the goose that laid the golden egg. So can SPAM, that e-box clutter that everyone despises.

Keep an open mind for promotion ideas: Look at the small details in your book. There will be angles there you can exploit when you're talking to editors. My book, *This is the Place*, is sort of romantic (a romance website will like it), but it is also set in Salt Lake City, the site where the Winter Games were played in 2002 and, though that's a reach, I found sports desks and feature editors open to it as Olympic fervor grew, and even as it waned.

Cull contacts: Develop your Rolodex by adding quality recipients from media directories. The website *http://www.gebbieinc.com/* has an All-in-One Directory that gives links to others such as Editor, Publisher Year Book, and Burrell's. Some partial directories on the web are free and so are your yellow pages. Ask for help from your librarian — a good research librarian is like a shark; she'll keep biting until she's got exactly what she wants.

Etiquette counts: Send thank-you notes to contacts after they've featured you or your book. This happens so rarely they are sure to be impressed and to pay attention to the next idea you have, even if it's just a listing in a calendar for your next book signing.

Partner with your publicist and publisher: Ask for help from their promotion department — even if it's just for a sample press release.

Publicize who you are, what you do: Reviews aren't the only way to go. E-books are big news right now. Katy Walls, author of *The Last Step*, coordinated an "anthology" of recipes from authors who mention food in their books (yes, some of my family's ancient recipes from polygamist times are in it). It is a free e-book, a promotional CD, and great fodder for the local newspapers. As a sample you can download it at *www.TLT.com/authors/ carolynhowardjohnson.htm.*

Think of all the angles. What if you're very young? What if writing a book is a new endeavor for you? Several editors have liked the idea that I wrote my first book at an age when most are thinking of retiring, that I think of myself as an example of the fact that it is never too late to follow a dream.

Develop new activities to publicize: Don't do just book signings. Use your imagination for a spectacular launch. Get charities involved. Think in terms of ways to help your community.

Send professional photos with your release: Request guidelines from your target media. Local editors won't mind if you send homey Kodak moments — properly labeled — along with your release. Some will use them; it may pique the interest of others and they'll send out their own photographers. However, do keep your photos professional for national or slick magazines, newspapers, etc.

Frequency is important: The editor who ignores your first release may pay more attention to your second or twenty-fifth. She will come to view you as a source and call you when she needs to quote an expert. This can work for novels as well as non-fiction. I received a nice referral in my local newspaper because I am now an "expert" on prejudice, even though my book is a novel and not a how-to or self-help piece.

Follow Up: Shel Horowitz, author of *Marketing Without Megabucks* (*http://www.frugalfun.com*), reports that follow-up calls boost the chances of a press release being published. Voice contact builds relationships better than any other means of communication.

Keep clippings: Professional publicists like Debra Gold do this for their clients; you do it so you'll know what's working and what isn't.

Evaluate: One year after your first release, add up the column inches. Measure the number of inches any paper gave you free, including headlines and pictures. If the piece is three columns wide and each column of your story is six inches long, that is 18 column inches. How much does that newspaper charge per inch for their ads? Multiply the column inches by that rate to know what the piece is worth in advertising dollars. Now add 20% for the additional trust the reader puts in editorial material.

Set goals: You now have a total of what your year's efforts have reaped. New publicist-authors should set a goal to increase that amount by 100% in the next year. If you already have a track record, aim for 20%.

Observe progress: Publicity is like planting bulbs. It proliferates even when you aren't trying very hard. By watching for unintended results, you learn how to make them happen in the future.

Carolyn Howard-Johnson is the author of *This is the Place* and
Harkening: A Collection of Stories Remembered
She has nearly three decades experience publicizing her own retail
business and was a fashion publicist in New York.

The Book is Out
D. A. Johnstone

When my first book was published, I wanted to stand out on Main Street and broadcast the news to the world. Not having the voice for it, I decided on other tactics. There was a July Fourth event in town, so I took a booth to sell the book. I was happy I had decided on a pseudonym, since I was a shy person and found it difficult to speak positively about my own work. Ann Doro, the name under which I write for children, helped. Because I could assume a different persona, I contacted local book stores and arranged for signings, then called the local radio station to be interviewed at Barnes & Noble during an autograph session. I sent press releases to the local papers, and was gratified when reviews of the book appeared.

Since it was a children's book, I contacted the librarian of the local elementary schools, and she arranged for me to speak in all the classrooms. At one school, I sat for well over an hour autographing books the kids had bought. I sought other invitations and traveled to a number of schools, both in my own area and in Southern California.

During that time I traveled a lot, visiting friends in Oregon and up and down California, and also flying to see my daughter in Florida. I went into every bookstore I saw, asking if they would stock the book. *Charlie, The Lost Dog*, was a great success, partly because I was eager to help promote it.

D. A. Johnstone (Ann Doro) is the author of *Trio* and
Charlie, The Lost Dog

Don't Give Up
Karen Kerr

"Do not give up," quotes Karen Kerr, author of *Seasons of My Life: A Personal Journal of a Breast Cancer Survivor*, published 2000.

And the beat goes on for this author's small published book. Since this book related feelings encountered throughout her breast cancer ordeal and since these are the 'times' that women are facing this unfortunate disease, nothing is more to the forefront than this topic.

These are nice words, but everyone can not be an instant "Harry Potter" author, so I felt that I needed to get on the bandwagon and promote.

Where to start? After I was accepted by PublishAmerica, I sent them 200-300 addressed mailing labels so they could get the ball rolling. I then talked to the editor of our local newspaper (two cities together of about 80,000 and out-lying towns) about my achievement. The Book Section editor conducted an interview with me, and I was in the Sunday edition with a large article!

I sent my book to three other major newspapers in Iowa, but only heard back from one, when they returned my book, as they receive over 100 books a week. I'll wait until October, as that is Breast Cancer Awareness month, and hit that paper up again. Perseverance, you see.

After the article came out, I had several calls from women's groups (health, social, educational, etc.) to do book signings and discussions.

My next endeavor was to contact the TV stations. One in particular did an interview (I also knew that gal as she had done lots of segments on a child in my school who had survived cancer). That went over really well, and, four months later, led to me doing another TV segment because I was the honorary chair for a Pink Ribbon Breast Cancer Golf Tournament. The same gal did that interview, too.

I sent informational data to all the hospital mammography units in our city, all the American Cancer centers in the US, and also to the breast cancer groups within those cancer centers. I will do a follow-up on all those this year, as I did not ask for any replies from them. I just felt that I needed to let them know that there is a simplistic book written by someone who has been through this ordeal and has survived.

Then I began getting correspondence by phone, e-mail, and written notes from individuals asking me to speak to their groups. Me? Speak? I took a deep breath and decided I DID believe in my work and I wanted to sell my book, so I had better get with the program! I accepted each one as it arrived. The first one was difficult, but I made it and because the audience asked questions I learned what to include to get prepared for the next speech. I learned to have a visual: a poster board with the information from those newspapers, where to get my book, and a picture and bio of myself.

I was a survivor. My product was about me. People like to hear about what others have to endure, so it became easier as the year went on. I was fortunate to get another interview with the same TV station to boost my book. It goes on and on, as does this disease, so my topic doesn't go away. The book is good for reading, and then to give as a gift.

I have two more ideas, as I'm always thinking of new, creative ways to promote. We are having a major book company coming to our city. I want my book on their shelf. I tried in the past, in another city less than 100 miles away, BUT some kind of jargon about having an agent or something is standing in my way. When this company opens their doors and begins to hire, I will go directly to the manager and see what can be done for it to be on the shelf. I am persistent, but I have my work cut out for me. My ploy will offer that I be at the store entrance to do book signings.

My second idea is to watch for *The Oprah Winfrey Show* topics and try to be on one of her shows which pertains to women's health.

I will persevere. I will not give up.

Good luck to all of you who are doing the same thing.

Karen Kerr is the author of *Seasons of My Life: A Personal Journal of a Breast Cancer Survivor*

Promoting Your Book in Local Magazines and Newspapers
Chris Lee

Obviously, the ideal way to promote a book is with a huge and expensive marketing campaign with several signings scheduled across the country, elaborate displays in every store, a series of radio and television commercials, reviews in several periodicals and newspapers, and a few television appearances on some major networks. A book with this kind of exposure is bound to do well, even if it stinks. On the other hand, if this is your first book, the local bookstores don't want to assume the financial risk of carrying it, and if you do not have a great deal of money or time to spend on promotion, marketing your book will be trickier — but not impossible.

Effective marketing can sometimes be a difficult concept for some people to grasp. It's good to be aggressive and proactive, but at the same time, you need to exercise proper discretion in how you present yourself and your book. I don't have a background in advertising, but I have studied social psychology. And whereas presenting your book in an aggressive but tasteful manner can surely help, an aggressive effort in a distasteful manner can hurt your cause and make you look like a hack. An example would be the massive amounts of e-mail advertisements, otherwise know as spam. I receive about twenty e-mail advertisements a day, and have never read any of them. Obviously, someone is being very aggressive as they send me e-mail after e-mail, but they are not having any effect on me whatsoever. I can also say the same for those pesky pop-up ads that appear when I surf the Internet, or those telemarketers who leave messages on my machine or call at the most inopportune time.

The bottom line is that when I need something, I go out and look for it. I don't pray for someone to save the day by sending me an advertisement. If an advertisement does grab my attention, it's because it was in something I chose to read or examine. That being said, one way I have chosen to present my book is in mediums where people have either requested or bought it. The most inexpensive way I have found to do this is in local periodicals.

Before your book is released, you should begin to put together a small press kit that introduces you and explains what your book is about. You want to give them adequate information, but you don't want to give them too much information or they might not get around to reading it all. The press kit I have developed has all of the normal stuff such as the title, ISBN number, contact information for me and my publisher, and price. But I have also included a synopsis of my book, background information as to how it was written, and a small biography. And as you write your biography, I would tie it in with how your life experiences led to the writing of your book.

I have also included two or three printouts of links where my book can be purchased through major retailers. If these pages just happen to contain good reviews from readers, that will help as well. (Try to get your friends and family to write as many good reviews as possible.) But even if these pages don't yet have reviews, I would include a couple of them anyway. Listing a few major retailers or booksellers who are carrying your book can give you instant credibility with the editor of a periodical. You should then collect this information in a plastic folder with a clear cover. This will look much more professional than just stapling or paper clipping the pages together. Ideally, each kit should not cost more than a dollar or so to assemble, making it a very inexpensive method of querying an editor.

Once you have assembled a press kit and have a few review copies of your book on hand, you are now ready to begin locating your local newspapers and magazines and developing a list of contacts. I would begin by contacting the Chambers of Commerce in all of the major cities in your area and requesting the contact information of all of the periodicals that are members.

You should also speak with the independent antique booksellers in these areas. Even though they probably won't be interested in carrying new releases, they can be an invaluable resource. If they have been in business a long time, they should have an idea of what the local book market is like. They might have even published a book or two themselves. They will probably be able to tell you about all of the periodicals in the area that might be interested in your book and the ones that are easiest to work with. They might also put you in touch with other local writers who can help you as well. If you do meet someone who is willing to offer this much help (as I did), I suggest that you give him or her an autographed copy of your book as a courtesy. You should also give them as much patronage as you can.

Once you have assembled your list, try to obtain a copy of each periodical and review their submission guidelines. E-mails and phone calls are probably acceptable (snail mail is too expensive), but I prefer to drop by in person. If you are lucky enough to meet an editor or a writer on a drop-in visit, and they are interested in your work, you can go ahead and leave a review copy with them as well as your press kit. But if you only have an opportunity to speak with a secretary or a member of the support staff, I would only leave a press kit at that time. Then if the editor decides he or she would like to review your book, or request an interview, you can then provide them with a copy. Otherwise, if the editor decides that he or she is not interested, you will most likely not get the book back.

There are many ways a book can be presented in a periodical. Obviously, an interview or a review is ideal, but you might also offer an excerpt. (Always consult your publisher concerning their policy on excerpts before you do this.) Another option might be to write an article for the magazine in exchange for an ad. It could very well be about how you were inspired to write your book, or it could be about anything. I once received a mention about my book in a periodical in exchange for a picture I had taken.

The main thing to remember is to be persistent, but professional. If a periodical doesn't want to do business with you, just move on and don't take it personally. Remember, someone thought enough of your book to publish it, which means that, with proper persistence, people should eventually think enough of it to buy it.

Chris Lee is the author of *College Planning in the Twenty-first Century: The Definitive Guide for College Students Who Want a High GPA, a Low Student Debt, and a Good Job After Graduation*

Tips on How to Sell Your Book
Ginny Lee

* In talking with others who may want to purchase your book, relax and be yourself so you can sell yourself in promoting your book.

* Instead of dressing casual, dress in your Sunday best. For instance, a dark suit or dress is much more appealing and professional looking when you meet in public to speak or to sell your book.

* Take an interest and listen to what others are saying to you. Be prepared to answer their questions. Don't be long and boring in your speech. Remember, a little goes a long way. Always smile; it will make people wonder what you are going to say next.

* Ask to see and talk with the mangers of bookstores. Have a copy of your book available to show to them. Tell them how and where your books are available for ordering. Be willing to have a book-signing party if possible. Put an article in your local newspaper about your new release.

* Have name cards printed in the form of bookmarks that will complement your book. Hand them out freely to anyone interested in your book.

Ginny Lee is the author of *Fireside Stories*

Techniques I Use to Sell Books
Lloyd E. Lenard

Some of the things I do as a writer to sell my books:

1. I'm proud of my published novels, and I pursue the sale of copies of both of them with unflagging zeal. If a writer isn't proud of his work, no one else will be.

How do I show this pride?

I make an opening to tell others each time I see someone. I have a business card printed in color with details about the book: the title, author's name, address and telephone number. It's a conversation starter. I hand it to them and say, "I think you'd be interested in my new novel, *Miracle on the 13th Hole*. It's an exciting story with tension, conflict, pace, and memorable characters. Many people who've bought it phone me to say, 'It's a page turner. I couldn't put it down.' It's available at Barnes & Noble and other fine bookstores."

2. The card is an excellent conversation starter. Usually, the people to whom I hand the card are strangers, and many of them are impressed by someone who has actually written a book and had it published.

3. I know. It does take "pushing myself out of my comfort zone," but how can people buy the book if they don't know about it? Besides, I've become obsessed with seeing sales of the book grow. That's why I wrote the novel. I wanted to see my name on the cover, touch it, turn the pages, revel in my success.

4. So, an author "must screw up his or her courage" daily, almost hourly. I seek out meetings to attend, restaurants where prospective buyers might go, church and Sunday School groups, civic club and service club meetings.

5. I must stay highly visible, enthusiastic, friendly, and eager to tell people about my work. It took months, sometimes years, to write the novels. It's a sizeable investment of the precious minutes of my life. I want others to know about the books and tell their friends. Yes, it takes courage, even brashness, to do this, but I've met some wonderful people and gained many new friends.

6. I belong to over a dozen civic and service clubs. I talk to the program chairman, knowing that such groups are always hungry for good programs. I sell the chairman on giving me a date so that my pretty, articulate wife and I can tell club members about the book. I find they're proud to have one of their members as a published author.

I start the program (a type of book review) telling them about the book. I interrupt my remarks to say, "Sky (that's my wife's name), read the part that tells about the struggle the chief protagonist, Dwight Church, is having with fighting off mid-life crisis and career burnout."

My wife then steps to the microphone and reads passages from the book. She's quite good and understands the work completely, since she serves as my editor and proofreader.

Then I step back to the microphone and tell a few additional things about the book, things that lead into my wife reading another passage from the book.

It's great fun. She and I jointly have planned and written out such programs, rehearsed them and are ready to present the club programs. Of course, we hand out the card I mentioned previously as a reminder for them to buy and read the novel, and then tell their friends about it. And we usually carry a few books with us, just in case they are anxious to buy one on the spot.

I was wise enough to write both my novels with specific markets in mind. *The Last Confederate Flag* expresses the philosophy on the flying of that honored banner as a salute to Southern cultural heritage. We've traveled the South making presentations and selling books to chapters of the Sons of Confederate Veterans and the United Daughters of the Confederacy. They result in many book sales. Since I'm a loyal member of SCV, I love this kind of thing.

As for *Miracle on the 13th Hole*, it has two great markets — the Christian community and the golfing fanatics. It's been easy to line up presentations to church groups and golfing groups and book clubs. Many book sales result.

7. Over a period of weeks, she and I mail out letters about the book, telling about its plot and memorable characters, where the novel is available and its price. We've compiled such mailing lists from friends, Christmas card lists, church and club rosters, and people we've come to know through the years. In each of them, we enclose the previously mentioned card, and ask them to buy and read the book and tell others about it. It works, and works very well. I tell them they can order the novel from me, and then I give the price and mailing costs. Or we tell them the name of a bookstore where they can buy it. Many times, we enclose copies of the promotional letter which PublishAmerica has sent out (I've had it copied at Office Max or Kinko's). I also enclose one of the cards about the book and a personal note in an accompanying letter. On the PublishAmerica promotional letter is a "special price deal" and an order blank. Many have told me they ordered the book through this means.

8. I choose 100 or more friends and good acquaintances. My wife looks up their phone numbers. I then telephone them with excitement in my voice and urge them to buy an autographed copy of the novel from me. It works quite well. Yes, it takes courage, but I wrote the novel, invested years of my life and I'm proud of it. People should buy and read it.

9. I hired a college student who's studying marketing, wrote a telephone script for her to follow, then got her to call each Barnes & Noble in ten states to urge them to stock the book. Of course, I rehearsed her on the phone talk, gave her answers to possible objections, and outlined for her that "you're in marketing and will be doing this kind of thing for a living." It has worked quite well.

10. I spend some part of each week endeavoring to line up bookstores for signings. Once we have such a date, I mail copies of the book's cover to the store, along with a one-page autobiographical sketch and a one-page summary of "What's the Novel All About?" It gets the bookstore buyer or community relations manager very interested.

I then send the store a sample press release, and urge them to give the book reviewer of the city's newspaper a copy of the book and a suggested "review/ press release." It helps, and, unless I do this, the chances of coverage are almost non-existent.

11. My wife and I prepare well for such signings. We "screw up our courage," have the handout cards ready and a review of the novel, and, when the store traffic comes flowing by, we boldly approach them, introduce ourselves and share our excitement over the book. We urge them to pick up the book from our table and read the jacket copy. We work such signings hard.

I've seen other authors at such signings actually sitting at the table reading a magazine. They never seem to look up. Yes, I know they're frightened to start conversations with strangers, but I look at them and sigh sadly for them. They're not selling their book and are obviously not proud enough of it to get excited. It's a tough, brutal world, but writing and selling our books is done in this kind of milieu. So, we try to cope with it.

12. No, my wife and I aren't geniuses. We get scared just like everyone else, but we are obsessed with selling our book. And the signing is over in two or three hours. We can endure "fire and brimstone" that long. After all, why did I write the book? Certainly not to die an anonymous death or stack up unsold copies in our storage room. No, that's an anathema to me and my wife.

And that's the kind of world I bargained for. I wrote the book, found an agent, the agent sold it to a publisher, and the publisher took a financial risk in printing copies. The least I can do is to try and sell it.

Lloyd E. Lenard is the author of *The Last Confederate Flag* and
Miracle on the 13th Hole

Promo Pointers
Laurie Lonsdale

Admittedly, I was somewhat timid at first with regard to promoting myself, and some of my reasons included that I didn't wish to appear obtrusive or boastful. I was uncomfortable to talk about my accomplishments, and I didn't want people to feel as though I was pressuring them to purchase my books. I soon came to realize that, more often than not, people were extremely interested to know that I was an author, and when I relaxed enough to speak about my works with the same kind of passion with which I wrote them, I saw that my enthusiasm was contagious and usually resulted in a sale. I now find it easy to talk about my books, and in addition to simply spreading the word by mouth, I have developed a number of different ways to promote them. My methods are as follows:

Before exiting a restaurant, I leave one of my bookmarks alongside my tip. Considering that they were designed to contain the book jacket, my name, the ISBN number, and all pertinent information with regard to where the book is available, as well as the back jacket synopsis, whoever picks it up will have all the data they need to pursue a purchase, should they find it interesting.

I never enter a bookstore without asking the manager if I can leave a stack of my bookmarks on the cash counter, either to be picked up by customers or handed out with purchases. I have yet to be denied, and considering that readers will use them in the books they have just bought, it's a great way to get them interested in my works as well.

Rather than pay my bills at the bank or online, I do it the old-fashioned way by check, so I can include a bookmark in the envelope.

While visiting a friend in the hospital one day, I came across a fund-raising book sale in the lobby. Seeing as I carry a bundle of bookmarks with me, I asked if they would like a stack to hand out with purchases, and they readily accepted.

Many restaurants have weekly draws for free lunches or dinners and use a glass bowl to collect business cards for the draw. With that in mind, I always leave my card (which includes my book titles, their ISBNs, etc.) Even if I don't win a free lunch, someone will read the card and may even pass it along.

As a big fan of my work, my hairdresser displays some of my books in her salon and promotes me in-store, telling her clients of my novels and selling copies whenever she can.

While getting this year's income tax prepared, I told the accountant about my books, and after my impassioned speech, he was moved to buy several copies which he now hands out to special clients as a "thank you" for their business. To others, he hands out my bookmarks.

For both my book releases, I approached several local newspapers and found that they were only too happy to write cover stories for their entertainment sections. I also approached a local television station, which gladly conducted a fifteen-minute interview and even followed me to a book signing for extra film footage.

Whenever I contribute an article or anecdote to a magazine, I also send in my by-line, which includes my book titles and their ISBNs.

In addition to setting up appearances at regular bookstores, I have even done a signing at a senior citizens' home where the residents didn't have access to the Internet to purchase books online and weren't able to get out to a bookstore or library. The last one I did was hugely successful (I sold 22 copies in two hours), and the residents were extremely grateful to be able to host the event. Always hungry for something new to read, they can't wait for my next book and have requested that I return.

At the conclusion of any of my bookstore signings, I ask the manager if I can leave behind a few books as well as my business card. I have learned that this is very effective, as many people are hesitant to impulse buy and need some time to think about their purchase. Others find book signings intimidating — even though they're interested, they're afraid to approach the table. By leaving copies with the store, this covers anyone who returns to buy my books after I have left, and in some instances I have received calls to replenish the stock.

I keep my websites fresh and link them directly to PublishAmerica and all online bookstores where my books can be purchased. I also join writers' clubs and associations so that my name and book titles will be listed on their sites as well.

I actively seek celebrity endorsements, making sure to enclose my bookmarks with my request. Whether or not the celebrity chooses to review my work, at least my name and book titles are on their lips, or at the very least, their agents'.

I had an attractive, re-useable banner made that includes my name and website, as well as the book jacket designs for my books, and use it at signings and festivals to attract attention.

I wrote to the supplier of the national library system, and after reading some online reviews of my books, they now distribute my works to their client libraries.

At all times I keep a few copies of my books in my car. That way I am prepared if I am approached by someone interested in purchasing my works.

I participate in book festivals and author gatherings as much as possible. Often these events are hosted by libraries and are an excellent and inexpensive way to network and spread the word.

And lastly, family, friends and fans are invaluable. The more people talking about my books, the better.

Laurie Lonsdale is the author of *Chasing Rainbows, Catching Dust* and *Neon Nights*

PublishAmerica Tips List
Steven Manchester

When promoting oneself as a published author, I'm certain that different approaches have worked for different people. I've also learned, however, that the only restrictions are found within the mind. The trick is to get yourself out there, constantly, and to be tenacious in your pursuit. Below are just a few of the practices that have worked for me over the past ten years.

My theories:
* PERSEVERANCE! If you forget every other word in the English language, hold on to perseverance. When it comes to marketing and promotion, it is the most important trait needed for success (more so than knowledge, talent or chance).

* Understand that success must happen within the mind before it can be realized. Trust that you will be (even are) a great success, and live up to that truth.

* Write down your goals, maintain a wish list, and work diligently toward them.

* Set VERY HIGH expectations for yourself, and do at least one thing every day toward realizing them.

* Create a network of readers and fellow writers, and watch the circle grow larger as they help you succeed. It's who you know! The most difficult path is trying to get things done without help.

* Be AWARE of opportunities all around you — big and small — and capitalize on all of them. Unless you're sitting at the poker table, you can't expect to get dealt a winning hand. Place yourself where you can meet opportunities.

* Though it sometimes takes years to become an overnight success, it doesn't pay to be shy. Be confident, but not cocky. This isn't a business for the overly humble.

* Successful marketing is like fishing: The more bobbers you have in the water, the better your chances of catching a string of fish.

* Become a zealous promoter of your published works, go to any lengths to capture success with each book, and be grateful to your loyal readers.

On the practical side:

* Create a website for yourself and promote it shamelessly. (See: *www.JacobEvans.com*)

* Volunteer your time (at literacy events, etc.), and read your work at open mics.

* Do the research, and use your competition as your ally. "A rising tide carries all ships." Readers are topical, staying with a specific genre. If they like a certain type of book, they'll read four or five before exhausting interest. More often than not, your competition is not your enemy but your ally.

* Attend other writers' book signings and readings. Offer a business card, and then ask for one. Introduce yourself, but don't take too much time. Follow the meeting up with an e-mail within the next few days (filled with compliments and your wishes of sharing contacts and networking). Don't be shy about asking for favors. Be equally willing to be of assistance.

* Use log lines: Write three or four sentences best describing each of your books, and memorize them. When asked what your work is about, recite these polished blurbs.

* Do as many author interviews as you can, and host as many local events as possible. (As a published author, it's not difficult to become a local celebrity.)

* Keep a close pulse on current events, and attach yourself.

* Set up book signings, saturating a specific area at one time (hence, a book tour). The average number of books purchased per signing is 20.

* Solicit celebrity (including other authors) endorsements.

* Ensure that your work can be purchased at Amazon.com and B&N.com. This automatically makes your work national.

* Get your books listed in the *Library Journal* (which is distributed to ALL libraries).

* Request magazines and newspapers to review your work. Many will.

* Contact your local media, via press releases. From there, build momentum by interviewing on local radio and TV.

* Embark on a national radio tour. This takes some research, but most radio programs are in constant search of new guests.

* Write a strong bio, and keep it updated.
* Promote your work via word of mouth, college circuit, speaking engagements at area schools, area book clubs (also, Rotary, Kiwanis, etc.), authors' associations and organizations (VFW, AGWVA, DAV, etc.).
* Capitalize on Internet connections where your work has been published. Also, promote your work on other websites by getting your site linked.
* Publicity/Promotions usually includes: A mass mailing of glossy postcards, and an equally heavy mailing of press releases.
* Throw a book release party and promote it! Your book is as big as you treat it, and others will follow suit.
* Try to hook up with an independent filmmaker to have your work filmed. This creates incredible hype on a local level!
* And whatever else you can imagine. THE SKY IS THE LIMIT!

Advice for new writers:
* Be true to yourself, always. Write constantly. Keep the faith!
* And NEVER, EVER, EVER quit. Most people in this industry would agree that more than talent or skill or even luck, perseverance is the one trait that gets the job done.
* Knock on every door you can, and keep knocking. I promise that eventually someone will open and the warmth you feel on your face will more than validate every hour spent alone in the darkness.

Steven Manchester is the author of *A Mother's Love*

Five Foolproof Ways to Get Your Book the Attention it Deserves

L.C. Martin

Send out a press release. This should be done just before your book hits the market. Send it out to news media, newspapers, libraries, local bookstores, and anybody else you can think of who may have an interest in your book. If it's a non-fiction book, then think about what type of groups and websites would be interested. For fiction, you may want to hit different websites that attract readers to their sites. For instance, if it's a romance novel, there are a number of romance sites that would be happy to post information about your novel, and also have you, as an author, featured on their site. Many of these sites offer author interviews as well. And just like a query letter, your press release has to grab the attention of the person who reads it. So make sure it's as polished and persuasive as it can be. There are a number of websites that have sample press releases.

Four elements of a good press release:

1. The heading. It should be one or two sentences that will pique interest and encourage the reader to finish the rest of the release.

2. Briefly describe what your book is about. One or two paragraphs. Make it compelling. You might also want to add a review blurb if you have one.

3. Include a brief and interesting paragraph about yourself.

4. Purchasing information. This should include your publisher's site, where to call to order your book, the ISBN number, and your contact information.

Pick up the phone. I found, by calling bookstores myself, I received more positive results than when I sent out e-mails and letters. This works especially well with libraries and independent bookstores. While an initial e-mail introducing yourself and your book is a good idea, it enforces your existence when you follow up with a phone call. Be persistent, but don't be a pest. If after e-mailing and a couple of phone calls you don't get results, then move on. It may be time consuming, but it actually works. In this day and age of technology, people still enjoy the human touch. Building relationships is what it's all about. When you do land that book event, and believe me, you will, make sure to send out a press release to the media regarding the event. You want as much press coverage as you can get. You may even get an interview, or be featured in the Books and Entertainment section.

Attend conferences and workshops. Networking is the best way to get the word out. At writers' conferences and workshops, not only do you meet fellow writers and learn ways to perfect your craft, but you'll have the opportunity to meet with agents and publishers as well. Make sure you have plenty of business cards with you. Many conferences are listed in *Writer's Digest*, which, by the way, every writer should have a subscription to. They always have great tips on promoting your work.

You need a website. This is important. It's a way to promote your book to millions of people. You can link your site to other sites, as well as give out information regarding your appearance schedule and upcoming books, post reviews, create a chat section, and so much more. You may even want to offer your own newsletter, which can be sent via e-mail. Always have your URL address and e-mail address listed on your business cards and bookmarks. These are two items that I strongly suggest investing in. It's an inexpensive way to get your name out there. I can't tell you how many times I've been discussing my book with someone, and when I hand them my card or bookmark, I usually get an e-mail back from them. Almost everyone can use a bookmark. I casually hand them out to people who are reading in the airport or by the pool. Earthly Charms does a great job with bookmarks for a reasonable price (*www.earthlycharms.com*).

Join a writing group. Surrounding yourself with other writers is the best way I know to keep the creative juices flowing, and a great way of getting more exposure. As a group, it may be easier to book events with bookstores, schools, and libraries, which may wish to have more than one author speaking. A panel is a good way to promote your work without seeming self-indulgent. Also, you can pool your money to obtain a booth at a local book fair or art festival. Some of the major book fairs maybe a little more expensive, but are worth every penny. If you can't find a group, then start one of your own, or join an online group. The exchange of ideas and networking is priceless, and, if you find the right group, it'll be one of the best experiences you will ever have as a writer.

L.C. Martin is the author of *Caught in the Rain* and *Destiny*

Trump for Success

Farzana Moon

There are several guides to promote one's book, but no special guideline to paint-by-number. The number one rule is to talk about one's book as if it is the only news worth sharing and circulating. This is also the first step in promoting one's book, a small one for sure, yet worth the gain and pleasure, considering that word of mouth travels faster than the magic in cyberspace.

Before taking a stroll down the avenue of dreams, or an abrupt leap towards the vistas of success, one must keep returning to the first step to explore the acronym "Aim To Succeed." A is for advertising with the candor of a tourist, calling the libraries and bookstores, and getting in touch with friends who might be interested in hosting social gatherings where signed copies could be made available with one flourish of the pen and a flash of smile.

T is for tobogganing down the slope of oblivion via e-mails and snail mails to selected targets of interest who might decide to purchase a copy, moved by curiosity, if not finding the title irresistible.

S is surrendering to the game of chance by doling out complimentary copies to the proud moguls of TV and radio, or even to celebrities with an optimistic flair to don the robe of visibility. Radio talks, TV interviews, guest at a local fair, etc.

If rejections surface with silences as deep as the night, trample them under your feet and pound them to dust before taking another slippery road toward the throne of recognition. Be patient and persistent, try again and again, and yet once again, sweeping away failures, inching closer to the mighty ranks in sales, which seem distant, but in reality are just around the corner. That corner is walled by books of different kinds, but your book stands out, holding its head high, peering above the multitude of the mundane and asserting its right to be the best.

It is the best, BEST, because you have made this declaration. B goes after

161

bravado, earning rank and recognition by the sheer will of one's own persistence. Don't dare ever give up! E is for earning respect, if not money, for the author's patience and hard work, so palpitating amongst the community of friends and relatives, are rewards worthy enough to cherish and cultivate. S and T revert back to the acronym mentioned earlier.

The Internet is a great tool, a place of gathering at the hearth of one's homepage, offering the rosary of camaraderie, inviting the strangers and stragglers alike to hum the gist of one's book and meditate upon the words, till their chants turn in favor of purchasing. One may never hear from anyone and think that no one visits, but the book is being noticed frequently by a diverse audience, growing in color and stature and rising above the waters of invisibility. My homepage, though designed by a friend, in addition to my inability to edit due to my computer illiteracy, has done wonders for me. Several students have e-mailed me requesting more information about the Moghuls or to use excerpts from my works in cyberspace for their thesis or dissertation. Cyberspace is a land of magic and miracles. One miracle winged its flight down my computer screen when Columbia University invited me for a humanities festival in honor of Salman Rushdie's play adapted from his book, *Midnight's Children*, in conjunction with Shakespeare's Theatre Company. My book, *Glorious Taj and Beloved Immortal*, beheld the light of ideation as I read one paragraph and talked about the Sufis and the Saints. With this miracle in hand and in deed, indeed! I must take shelter against the aura of the Sufis, invoking their blessings for more miracles.

Another miracle unfolds, one's own personal labor of love. One has written a book, and that's a miracle in itself. Keep it alive by the breath of promo. Even one single copy sold in a succession of lengthy interludes, something like the caprice of a crazy cloud, might generate a flood. Transforming "the sprinkling of rain" into a torrent, filling the lands and the oceans with its waters of hope and prosperity.

A few sprinkling of raindrops invoked by my own need to promote *Glorious Taj and Beloved Immortal*. My first step toward this goal was to call the local newspaper, informing the editors about the release of my book. One editor published a grand article in the local newspaper along with my photo, introducing me as an integral part of the community, whose book brought luster to art and culture in Springfield. The second step was a small one too, visiting the bookstores and requesting them to stock a few copies of my book. The manager at B. Dalton was very kind in displaying my books at the store in the Springfield Mall. Another little step, and the Springfield library invited the friends of the library to hear me read excerpts from *Glorious Taj and Beloved Immortal* and to talk about the Moghul history. Then Edison College in Piqua, Ohio, extended an invitation. A booth was set for me with posters and balloons, and my books were displayed for sale. They had also published my bio and photo in their paper, *Clear Creek Farm*. Those giant strides somehow learned the art of leaping, hurling me toward New York at Columbia University as mentioned earlier.

In conclusion, one must request friends to write reviews online, as soon a one's book is exposed to booksellers in cyberspace. The reviews should highlight the choicest morsels of interest, luring a diverse audience, almost screaming, "Buy me. Read me." A great challenge it is to be an author, greater yet to lend life support to one's creative child, but the greatest of all challenges is to keep plodding after the rungs of success and promotion. One step at a time! Erecting the mansion of ideas. Innovating and exploring. Shuffling the cards of chance, and aiming toward the domino effect in sales and promotion. Finally, I wish all authors the Trump of Success.

Farzana Moon is the author of *Glorious Taj and Beloved Immortal* and
The Moghul Exile

Use Your Expertise

Don Morse

Every book has at least one major theme. You're either an expert in that theme, or become an expert as the result of your research. You should use your expertise for marketing. I've written fifteen books, twelve of which are non-fiction. The first non-fiction was on root canal therapy, the second and eighth were on stress in dentistry, and the ninth was on oral/systemic health. I marketed those books primarily to dentists. The third non-fiction was a general book on stress. Since almost everybody is stressed, this book had a large potential audience. My fourth and seventh non-fictions were related to stress with women. Here, too, there was a vast potential audience. My fifth and sixth non-fictions dealt with stress and nutrition. Since stress is widespread, and everyone eats, the audience is obvious. My tenth and eleventh non-fictions were illustrated books on humorous animal sayings. Here, the main audience was children and people learning English as a second language.

Each of my fiction books had one principal theme. In *Deadly Reaction*, the lethal toxin was puffer fish poison. So, I learned about this poison. In *Eye to Eye*, the victims had a voodoo-like death. Hence, I learned about voodoo death. In *Lethal Penetration*, the victims died from vampire-like bites. I therefore researched vampirism. My newest novel is *Malpractice*. I've been an expert witness in dental malpractice cases, and learned about malpractice from lawyers.

For my dentistry-related books, I primarily marketed the books to the dental field. I gave my publishers contact information for dental schools, dental societies, and dental journals. I personally contacted individuals in the dental schools, societies, and in practice to let them know about my book. In addition, whenever I lectured throughout the Americas and in overseas countries, I had books available to sell and/or contact information about where the books could be purchased. Hence, my books were sold to dental school libraries and dental society headquarters and were adopted as textbooks by some dental schools. My books were reviewed by all major dental publications, and this helped sell the books to individual dentists.

For the trade books on stress, I was available whenever the publisher arranged for appearances on radio or television. However, even with large publishers (Van Nostrand Reinhold, Charles C. Thomas), that was a rarity. Hence, I contacted all the Philadelphia and South New Jersey radio and television stations and newspapers. Since stress was, and still is, a hot topic, and I was a professor at a major university, it was easier for me to gain access to those media outlets. I received many interviews and *The Philadelphia Inquirer* and *The South Jersey Courier Post*, among many other New Jersey newspapers, gave the books favorable reviews. In addition, Van Nostrand Reinhold was able to get my two best-known stress books (*Stress for Success*, *Woman Under Stress*) reviewed by the *Library Journal*, and both received high recommendations. This helped sell the books to libraries.

From the late 1970s onward, I've been a member of The Greater Philadelphia Society of Clinical Hypnosis and was President of that organization from 1983-1985. Since hypnosis and meditation are intriguing to the media, this helped me get interviews. I always mentioned my books on stress, which included discussions about those modalities. If the interviewer failed to mention the books, I politely asked him/her if I could mention the book and tell the listener/viewer how to obtain it.

Even before you go on the air, you should politely ask the interviewer if he/she could mention the book and tell how it can be purchased. Since you are not paid for being on the shows, and the subject matter is of interest to the listener/viewer, almost all hosts are pleased to mention, and even discuss, your book. With respect to that, make sure that the host has obtained a copy of your book at least two weeks before the scheduled appearance. Many of them do not read the entire book, but this gives them an opportunity to at least scan it.

My book, *Searching for Eternity*, was related to spirituality, which triggered interviews on spirituality and religion. To help sell my animal humor books, I gave talks in schools.

With my fiction books, I was able to get on radio and television and get print interviews because I emphasized the interesting themes in each book.

Wherever I travel, I try to get an interview with local media. To let them know when I will be in their area, I either telephone, e-mail, or snail mail ahead of time. This got me media interviews in San Francisco, Los Angeles,

New York, Philadelphia, Chicago, Ft. Lauderdale, and Miami. What is even better is to go to the area where part of your book takes place. For example, in *Deadly Reaction*, there are trips to Florida; in *Eye to Eye*, there is a trip to New Orleans; and in *Lethal Penetration*, there are trips to South Jersey and Philadelphia. This facilitated interviews in those regions. *Malpractice* takes place in South Jersey, Florida and Costa Rica, and I am preparing for interviews in those places. Finally, to keep calm, I use relaxation techniques (meditation, self-hypnosis, deep breathing) prior to any talk or interview.

With my stress books and fiction, I went to the managers of the local and regional book stores, told them who I was and what my book was about, and was able to get orders and book signings in Barnes & Noble and Borders, as well as other book stores. I also gave talks at local libraries and to societies and groups related to the specific topics in my books.

Become an expert and use your expertise to market your book.

Don Morse is the author of *Malpractice*

Use Your Resources
Lila B. Mullins

Promoting your book can be frustrating, to say the least. However, if done thoughtfully and carefully, it can be rewarding.

My first two books were non-fiction Christian inspirational. A small bookstore, relatively speaking, advertised my first book on a marquee that could be seen for several blocks. This bookstore also placed notices in their monthly statements.

Many booksellers have monthly newsletters and are willing to advertise your book, especially if they have offered to have a signing for you.

The best approach to booksellers is to call and ask what their procedure is for handling your book. Some require an application; others ask you to bring your book for reading by a committee or a designated person.

Florists that also sell gift items will occasionally display your book, and some shops will offer a signing.

As soon as possible, send a copy of your book to the book reviewer of *The New York Times* with a cover letter. Also send copies to several major newspapers in large cities.

Garden clubs, coffee clubs, book clubs, and other organizations of this type are often willing to promote your book. Consider giving your book as a door prize to suitable events.

College and university bookstores and libraries are good places to advertise your book to different age groups. Most assisted-living places have libraries where residents and visitors can choose reading material.

Geographical regions sponsor book festivals yearly; for instance, the Southern Book Festival takes place every October in Nashville, Tennessee. It is held in the city library and extends to the state museum or nearby public buildings. Authors read from their works and discuss with the public how and why their book was written.

Posters are valuable. Ask the booksellers who stock your book if you may place a poster in windows and inside. The poster should have a picture of the author, a short bio, a picture of the book cover with a short synopsis of the story, and the date and time of signing, if applicable. The booksellers will be happy to make a display of your book several days before the signing, because they want it to be a success as much as you.

Other businesses such as grocery stores, drug stores, florists, beauty shops, and clothing stores *may* permit a poster to be placed in their windows.

Ask friends and acquaintances for suggestions. They may have ideas you haven't thought about.

Local TV personnel usually will give an interview after reading your book. If you know someone connected with a particular channel, it may help.

Public speaking is easy for some people. They appear to have a natural ability; however, they may have worked very hard to overcome nervous tension. My best advice is "forget yourself — concentrate on your subject matter." You have a captive audience and they are anxious to hear what you have to say. This may seem simple, but it has worked for me. Now I'm anxious to speak, and I enjoy it. Remember that you are talking about your creation, and you will soon get lost in the story and completely forget yourself, and your audience will be spellbound.

As far as getting a signing in a university bookstore, you might think that would only be open to the university's published faculty or published alumni. However, if you check with the manager you might find that he or she would be willing to stock your book and eventually reward you a signing.

Lila B. Mullins is the author of *When the Sails Go Up and the Waves Come Ashore* and *Wind Out of the West*

Now I What?

Elizabeth Pezold

There is background music. Soft strains of "Maybe This Time" waft dreamily by your ear. A crescendo builds up and....

Sorry, I think I've been watching too many romance movies.

The day you have been hoping for arrives. You turn on your computer and...hallelujah!

"Congratulations, we are going to publish your book!"

You jump up and down and scream a lot. Luckily, you are alone in the neighborhood today. Then you call your husband at work and say slyly:

"How would you like to be married to a published author?"

His incredulous response is:

"You mean they are really going to publish it?"

Well, thanks a lot, dear, you think. Then he gets excited:

"Oh wow! Congratulations!"

By the time he gets home from work, everyone at the company has the word; his wife has a book being published.

Your husband looks at you at dinner and asks tentatively:

"Um, how is this going to affect our lives now?"

Is the status quo put askew, or can he remain in his anonymous comfort zone?

"Oh, I imagine things will be the same as before," you say comfortingly.

He looks dubious. A "public wife" is a new experience for him.

The experience is also new for you. Now what?

The next phase involves your final approval of the book text, and a really cool book cover. You fill out the required form from the Internet and send off for a copyright. Eventually, YOUR BOOK (sound of trumpets blaring) is delivered to your front door.

You immediately autograph all your copies.

That was the easy part. They don't tell you about author envy.

I went into a Barnes & Noble bookstore where a couple of ladies had set up a table with books. They were happily autographing away. I bought one of their books, appropriately written on the topic of promoting a published book. I sat down to read. (At home, of course — Barnes & Noble has a closing time.)

Several hours later, or maybe it was days, my neglected-feeling family gave a sigh of relief. I had a packet with flyers, bookmarks, an author questionnaire with answers, and an appropriate promotional letter to the newspaper, bookstore, and public personality of choice — whomever. I reminded my family and friends *my book* was now out. I think some of them threw out the promotional postcard sent by the publisher. At any rate, they still didn't know about the book.

The letters and packets to Barnes & Noble and other bookstores were returned in the mail. The reply:

"We are sorry but we don't stock print on demand books because we can't send them back to the publisher if they don't sell."

Humph!

They also said not to come in with an armful of books yourself and ask to set up here.

Double Humph!

Maybe I need to pay a personal book promoter.

This book is a valuable, enjoyable contribution, my heart cries in protest. Why doesn't anybody want my book? Notice that I take this very personally.

I wonder what Oprah's phone number is?

My church graciously agreed to let me put up a table and sell some copies there. Unfortunately, I have moved two hours north, and can't be there. We put up posters and tell them the books will be a contribution toward the church building fund. That will bring them in. I guess it did. They didn't send any books back, and maybe some were ordered online as a result. I was afraid to ask if the pastor just bought all the copies and stuffed them in a back room. (I seriously doubt it.)

The idea is to get your book "out there," right?

I have given them away as gifts to the police department.

I've seriously considered sending 300 copies to the Southampton Library anonymously. After all, the book does take place in Southampton. Unfortunately, that is an expensive plan. I haven't done it yet.

I sent a packet to a public personality, asking where to send him a personal copy of my book. I was getting low on books, so I didn't include it this time.

I received a nice letter back, informing me the gentleman didn't publish books. For crying out loud, the book is already published! I figured he would read it and put me on television. Sigh, I was foiled again.

I gave my child's teacher a copy at the end of the school year. She was delighted and said:

"I didn't know you were an author!"

"Apparently," I responded.

She laughed and told her class:

"We know someone famous!"

I was really sorry to tell her otherwise. At least she didn't ask:

"Where were *you* on career day?"

Notice that I have not given up. There is an advertisement for my book at the end of my child's school yearbook. An entire school could potentially check it out.

> *Proverbs 16:3 says "Commit to the Lord whatever you do,*
> *and your plans will succeed."*

Elizabeth Pezold is the author of *In His Time*

Crowds of People Flock to My Signings!

EJ Phillips

It is the norm that I sell from 15 to 45 books at each of my signings.

I have a built-in marketing plan by the very nature of my book: *WOMAN: What She Has Done With Where She Has Been.*

WOMAN is an anthology of stories about contemporary women who have overcome adversity — who have picked up, wiped their tears and gone on to build new lives.

I planned signings and appearances in the home area of each woman featured in *WOMAN* and I connected these appearances to an already scheduled event. I invited the women featured to join me at the signings. So at each appearance they not only visited with friends and relatives who stopped by to see them, they signed — and sold — books as well.

At a Texas-style barbeque in a little town in the Texas panhandle (population 47), we signed and sold 27 books.

At a Hoot-n-Scoot celebration in southwestern Oklahoma, we sold 15 books. (What goes on at a Hoot-n-Scoot? I have no idea. I was too busy signing and selling books, as well as autographing books sold prior to our scheduled appearance, to take in any of the activities.)

In southwestern Kansas, at the family gathering of one of the women featured, we sold 38 books.

And there was the time that I created my own event when I invited all the women featured in *WOMAN* to an all-expense-paid weekend at a bed and breakfast. It was the first time that most of them had met. We had a wonderful time getting acquainted, sharing stories, tears, and laughter, as well as signing each other's books. The women became hostesses, serving coffee, tea, fruit, and cookies to the townspeople who packed into the cozy living room of that

B&B. And the people came. They took snapshots…and they bought 45 books.

Twice, I scheduled signings at gift shops — each located in a small town. At the first signing, 24 books were sold and a repeat visit scheduled. At the second, 15 were sold.

None of these happenings took place in large cities. I've found that people who live in small towns often are hungry for "culture" and "celebrities." At each of the public events, I had people amble by who didn't know the person featured or me, but thought the book looked or sounded interesting so they bought.

There are other opportunities. One never knows who might be interested in buying or selling books. Ask!

I left 15 at a café located in a small town in northeast New Mexico, one of our usual stopping places for a bite to eat when traveling that direction. Those 15 sold almost immediately and the gift shop manager has placed an order for more.

I sold 20 to a high school friend who gave them to other classmates. She was proud of a fellow classmate who became "famous."

Certainly, I had an advantage because of the built-in audience of friends and family of the people featured in *WOMAN*. That's what marketing is — taking advantage of an advantage.

EJ Phillips is the author of *WOMAN: What She Has Done With Where She Has Been.*

Community Connection
Lila L. Pinord

What I did was very simple. We are a small town with three local bookstores. I went to each store and they looked at my book (I gave one to the owner). They ordered a few copies. I think the best method I found was to get in touch with two alma maters and ask if they would include me and my just-published novel in their quarterly publications. Both agreed. The articles will be in their fall editions.

I have a slight advantage in the fact that I am Native American. I e-mailed my former tribe and they immediately did an article in the tribal newspaper. I realize not everyone can do this. I also made up business cards and everyone I know got one: friends, relatives, doctors and nurses. My optometrist bought my book. I get such a wonderful response locally. Now I am going to have a PR person do what she can for me soon.

Lila L. Pinord is the author of *Skye Dancer*

First Impressions and Beyond

Joyce Rapier

An author's media review success amounts to perseverance on the part of the author. Before your book is published, contact the features editor of your local newspaper. Schedule a meeting, convenient with the editor, to introduce yourself. Make certain you have a neatly typed bio and brief description of your book(s). Always have decorum be the positive approach in relating or selling the value of your book. Smile and know you are worthy of being an author. Before you have the scheduled meeting, casually go inside the building and observe the dress code. Dress accordingly. First impressions are lasting impressions — you can dress down but never dress up after the first eye contact. Extend a greeting handshake and also a thank-you handshake when the interview is completed.

Pitfalls to avoid:

1. Keep appointments! If you miss an appointment, you won't be given another chance. Most editors feel pressured, to say the least, with all the responsibilities of their job. If they take the time to schedule an appointment with you — keep it. Perhaps in a family emergency, an editor would understand, but don't count on it. Never take anything for granted.

2. Respond to questions with certainty and never say the words, "I don't know." Refrain from using the pausing words or representative "hiccup" phrases such as Er, Uh, Well or Let me see, while in mid-sentence. Never approach an editor with, "I had a book published." They do not care. Many people have books published. If you *demand* coverage for your book, rest assured, you will not receive it.

3. Never go to an appointment with gum, candy or other edibles in your mouth. Whatever you do — brush your teeth. Don't laugh — no one wants to see anything sticking between the teeth or breathe garlic or onions.

4. Do not go to an appointment without being prepared. Take along a brief bio; when I say brief, I mean brief! No editor will read through mounds of accomplishments, regardless of how impressive they are. You are there for one purpose — your book. Should an editor ask other pertinent questions regarding your expertise of writing, don't say "I didn't bring anything to show." Have those papers or references neatly tucked away inside a notepad.

5. If you are asked what your book is about, don't merely say "roses," tell them about those roses and why, when and where you came to be so ardent about the content of your book. Any editor can pick up your book and look at the title. He/she wants *you* to tell them why you feel it would be of interest to the public.

BOOKSTORES:
If anything in the world can bring you down a notch or two, it will be a brick-and-mortar national chain. Most any reputable bookstore will automatically say the word "no" if you request a signing in their store. Managers are geared to the protocol of their company rules and can be very hard-nosed when approached. Generally, a manager wants to acknowledge you as being a "new writer," but quite frankly, they see dozens of writers a day.

DON'T lose faith or be disheartened. Speak to the manager and tell him/ her that you will supply the books for your signing. *YES*, you will have to purchase the books from your publisher, and *NO,* you can't return them! Most times a bookstore will only let you do the signing for a percentage of the take. Usually, 30% is what they prefer. GET IT IN WRITING — with a signature. People forget what they say and when they said it. It will be up to you to follow up with a confirmation for the signing.

THIS is the kicker! If you have trouble getting into a chain store, go to a mom-and-pop store, or an off-the-beaten-path bookstore. They are happy to help out a struggling writer and like to have customers coming into their store. They also require a percentage. If you are lucky enough to have a signing in the store, take the owner/manager a bouquet of flowers on your signing day. It will cement a bond between the two of you. Follow up with a thank-you note expressing your gratitude.

NERVES:
Yes, you will be nervous, have a hard time swallowing and want to run for the nearest exit, but remember — they know you are nervous. Break the ice

and say, "I am so nervous but it's from the excitement of being a new author." They will understand, and if they don't, forget it! Everyone gets nervous. It's how you handle the situation that counts.

HANDOUTS:

Don't go overboard with too many items — it becomes too costly for a struggling author. Begin with pens or bookmarks, and see if they will generate sales. Place a bookmark inside your books and give those away with the sale of a book. You will soon know—if you have many items left over—if handouts are for you. If handouts are a success, go with mouse pads or another type of personal computer item that will be noticed each day.

CELEBRITY STATUS:

Word of mouth and newspaper articles soon boost your morale. You suddenly have people phoning you for book signings. Libraries, schools and other management seek you out for speaking engagements. Complete strangers ask you to write their book or guidance for "how to" in finding a publisher. My response: Go to *publishamerica.com.*

Joyce Rapier is the author of *Windy John's me 'n tut* and
Windy John's, Rainbow and the Pot of Gold

Tips on Promoting Your Novel and Yourself
Dana Reed

After selling my first novel, I was pretty green when it came to publicity. So, I had my family and friends go to bookstores in the local mall and ask for my novels repeatedly until the owners/managers stocked them. By the time I sold the third, I was into making up press packets to send to local newspapers and radio stations.

One of the newspapers in my area, that covered most of Southwest Florida, sent a reporter to my home to interview me due to the packet they received containing copies of the book cover, a short bio on me, and information about my publisher. The editor of the Lifestyles section of that same paper decided to grant me a front-page story, complete with an elaborate color photo taken by one of their photographers. The photographer wanted to bring out the horror aspect of my novels, so he purchased masks of ghouls and so on, then created a picture where they circled my head in a kaleidoscope effect.

When the article was released, I was called by the person responsible for author coverage at one of the local TV stations. She granted me a fifteen-minute TV interview, and asked that I show all three of my novels. This led to an hour-long radio interview and several requests from libraries, bookstores, and author groups for both book signings and speeches on how to write a horror novel, and how I researched my novels. I was also contacted by the editor of the local newspaper, who asked if I'd like to do a weekly column, using my pen name. I agreed. All of this helped not only to promote the third novel, but the rest as they were released.

Public speaking can establish you as an authority on the subject of your novel, if you're careful to work with notes. Referring to your notes helps when you're nervous and your mind goes suddenly blank due to that nervousness. You should also be more than familiar with the subject. I say this because most of the readers who purchased my novels were intelligent — not because they bought my books, but because they were well versed when it came to Satanism, witchcraft, Ouija boards and many of the occult topics covered in my books. You can't fake it when you come in contact with modern-day druids, high priests and so on.

I was not in favor of these topics and wrote my novels with cautionary messages, so that people would stay away from them. As a result, most of the time I'd wind up in a debate with some members of the audience who took offense to my negativity, and this can happen to anyone, no matter what the subject of their material. Therefore, I caution you to remain calm, and don't fall into their trap. These people tried to develop a heated argument so that I'd look like a fool and ruin my credibility. Since I continuously took charge by maintaining my cool, they soon gave up.

The first time I was asked to speak in public, I was frightened to death. I've always been outgoing, but mainly with small groups of people. This was different: I was about to address an audience of about forty or fifty, sometimes more. But then I realized that I was asked to speak because I was a published author. This put me way ahead of a lot of members of the audience. They felt I had something interesting to say or they wouldn't have asked me. That knowledge helped quell those nerves.

I practiced beforehand by speaking in front of a mirror. I also got a few of my friends together and practiced on them. I told them to ask me questions about my novels. And, for friends, they were a tough crowd. They gave it to me. By the time I got up in front of my first audience, I couldn't help but smile because my friends were not there, if you get my drift. Public speaking gets easier as it goes along, and the same applies to book signings.

When you do your first book signing, notes help because people will question you at this event as well. They'll want to know how you chose this particular subject to write about, how you actually wrote the book, and if this is a one-time thing, or will you continue to write.

All in all, most of the people I've met over the years were wonderful to me. Most of them gave me hope, encouragement, and made me promise I'd never stop writing. So don't give up if you run into a few negative readers. Just remember, you can't please everyone, but if you can please mostly everyone, you're on your way to a whole new career as a serious author.

I'm about to have my tenth novel released in print, and have written three more that are ready for publication. Never give up, because writing novels and promoting yourself gets easier as you go along.

Dana Reed is the author of *Grave Results*

How I Marketed My Book

Connie Ann Rhineheart

In May of 2002, my book, *Miracles*, was published. It was suggested by PublishAmerica that I get business cards and a website established to help advertise my book. My business cards gave the information needed for customers to place orders. When I paid my bills by mail, I would place one of my business cards in the envelope with the bill. I also included my website address on the business cards. The webpage included excerpts from some of the stories that I had written in *Miracles*. My website, later without pop-ups, also included an e-mail address.

In June of 2002, I had to have emergency surgery. While I was in the hospital, I showed my book to everyone that came into the hospital room. I told them about the abusive life I'd had, and how God had set me free. Many people asked me for my business card, and I gave it to them. One nurse bought a copy of my book.

Wherever I would go, I always had one of my books with me. Most of my customers were very impressed with it, and wanted to know if I was going to write another book related to my first. I informed them that I was in the process of writing another book called *Walking in the Now*.

Once I was out of the hospital, I started going to a writers' group in my county. They told me that there was a bookstore in our county that would display books written from local writers. I talked with the owner of that bookstore about displaying *Miracles*. She took ten of my books on consignment. Then, in February 2003, I had a book signing at her store. While I was there, I had the opportunity to speak with customers and give them descriptions of the subject of my book. Since I am well-known at our local newspaper, because of placing ads and doing photography for some of the employees for my animal photography business, I found out, through a representative, that the paper did book reviews for new writers who lived in the county. So, in September of 2002, I went to the newspaper office to give my book to the editor to read.

At the end of September, I received a phone call from the reporter asking me to come in for an interview. It was a success! The article was published in the paper on September 28. I e-mailed this article to PublishAmerica so they could put this book review on their website. I made sure to include my website address in the book review that was printed in the paper. By having my website address in the article, people were able to contact me.

While I was at a Christian Women's Conference in North Carolina, I met a woman who told me about the terrible divorce she was going through. I then told her about my book that I had written, and how I felt that *Miracles* would help her. Because of her situation, I gave her a free copy of my book. After she had read my book, she phoned me to tell me how *Miracles* had blessed her. She also told me that she had loaned my book to her Christian counselor. She said that the counselor read my book, and was very impressed. She wanted to buy three copies so she could loan them out to her patients. This woman also told me that she wanted to pay me for the book I had given to her, and that she wanted to buy another copy of it.

Even though I had sold *Miracles* to many people, I ready didn't understand how to truly market it. I was out in the yard one day, when a neighbor, that I had sold one of my books to, happened by. She told me that I needed to get my book out to clinics that dealt with abused women. I told her that I didn't know how to accomplish that task. She told me that she would help me out, since her company specialized in marketing.

She suggested that I needed a different type of business card, one that gave my real name (as I had used a pen name to write the book), phone number and e-mail address. Also, under my name, it read: Published Writer, Speaker and Animal Photographer. Below this were two websites. One said: Published Works. The other one said: Photography Portfolio.

She also suggested that I needed postcards to send to the different abuse centers. On one side of the postcard was as a picture of a dying tree that had new growth coming back on it. Next to that tree were words describing my life. On the other side was a photograph of me and information on how the shelter could get in touch with me so I could speak at their center. (In speaking to groups of abused people, the main goal was to somehow help these people deal with their pain. However, a secondary goal was to spread the word about my book.)

My neighbor also suggested that I get involved in the community. I sold my books and photographs at the art-and-craft show in town. While I was there, I noticed a booth set up to inform people about how an abused women could get help. I told them how I was abused and how I had dealt with my past and was set free from it. They asked me if I would come to their shelter and speak to the abused woman there. This became another avenue for me to let people know about *Miracles*.

I am learning that marketing is an ongoing, ever-changing process. Every door that opens will in turn open others. The key is to constantly keep opening those doors!

Connie Ann Rhineheart is the author of *Miracles*

Network is the Key Word
CV Rhoades

Having written and published four books, soon to be five, I have learned a lot about promoting. Even though traditional publishers brought out three of the four, I still found myself having to promote. A lot. So far my best-selling book, *Strike Like Lightning, Meditations on Nature for Martial Artists*, was the one I promoted the most. I went to martial-arts tournaments to sign books, and sent copies to many of the masters in my federation. It all helped.

INTERVIEWS: For one thing, I did networking, and still do. I was a member of a writers' group for years, and my contacts there have helped greatly. One friend is my publicity agent; she does my interviews and turns them in to the local newspaper. Another friend does a radio show, and he mentions my books there.

Not being shy, I call the local radio station's morning talk show and tell them I would like a spot to promote my book. They have always been good at scheduling me. Of course, I live in a small town, and if I don't know them personally, I at least know who they are, and they know my name as well. This helps. Network is the key word.

Before your book is published, make an effort to find out the AM talk shows and the local television programs. I appeared on one with my first book, and I enjoyed it. Find out who is in charge of the talk show, and address your call or query to them. Most are looking for good copy.

BOOKSTORES: Here, again, network. I am well known to all the local bookstores, and those in the outlying areas. I simply ask for the person who is in charge of autograph parties and ask them to set me up. As a writer, you should be well known to your local bookstore already, so this part is the easiest. I read a good tip from one author, which I plan to try. As bookstores get books at 40%, and it costs something to return them, if the publisher takes returns, the author set up with the bookstore to buy the leftover books after the autograph party for 40% off. As most publishers do not pay royalties on books sold at author discounts, he made the bookstore happy, got more books, and got his royalties on those books. A win-win situation.

OTHER PLACES TO SELL BOOKS: If you have a specialized book, as mine are, find something in the town to tie in with your autograph party. I sold many copies of one of my books at martial-arts tournaments. If you write about writing conferences, contact a local writers' group, find out when the conference is, and set up a signing there. Main character a photographer? Check with photo studios about hosting a signing. (Of course, you have to buy the books, but I have found this a great way to get your name out and sell books.)

Libraries will often host a signing, many times in conjunction with a local bookstore. Call them and find out. Librarians and bookstores should know you in your area, and this makes it easier to make a connection.

PUBLIC SPEAKING: I have never been shy about public speaking, but many people are. If you are, just having something important to say can help a lot. Practice in front of family and friends, and in front of a mirror. Try a practice run in front of a few friends. Maybe read them some snippets of your work. Trust me. If you have the right friends (this is no time to invite those who may be jealous of your success), they will love it.

I have given talks on many subjects in front of many groups, and it gets easier every time. Just make sure you are well prepared, and don't ramble on too long. Twenty minutes plus a question-and-answer session is long enough.

HANDOUTS AND CARDS: Handouts can be helpful, and you should have a business card listing your book(s). I have printed up my own cards, and hand them out. For one thing, the cards include the names and where to purchase all my books; I hope for additional sales that way.

CELEBRITY STATUS: I have been a local celebrity for many years. I have written columns for newspapers where my photo appeared, and, believe me, everyone knows who I am. This is good and bad, but it sure helps when I have to sell books.

CV Rhoades is the author of *Beyond the Black Belt*

Marketing Strategy
Andrew F. Rickis

I believe the marketing strategy should begin before the writing process starts and certainly during the writing of a book. A story has to be exciting, and well developed with interesting characters to be successful. If these elements are missing, the book will not sell well over a period of time. Think and plan before and during writing.

One of the most important aspects of a successful book is the cover. Many potential buyers of a book will pick up and look at a book simply because the cover is attractive to them. *Use lots of color.*

Once the book is published, then the real work begins. Scan local newspapers and write or e-mail a short query note to article writers in these papers and ask if they would be willing to write an article about you and/or your book. Use the same approach with radio announcers for a live or recorded interview. *Be aggressive.*

Visit the small bookstores in your area and see if they would be willing to stock your book. Some may pay you up front or be willing to take your book on consignment. *Be persistent.*

Send book-release notices to everyone you know. I did this with my Christmas card list. *Or use e-mail.*

Organize a book fair with other local writers. Promote the event with radio announcements and newspaper announcements. *Put up posters of the fair all over town.*

Approach bookstores and libraries and convince them to do a book signing. Promote the signing like the book fair. *This can also be successful with a fellow author.*

And most important of all, ***never give up***.

Andrew F. Rickis is the author of *The MagicOak*

Get Back to the Basics
Barbara J. Robinson

Get back to the basics of good old-fashioned letter writing and pen your way to marketability. Write to hometown people you knew in the past and tell them about your newest book and writing success. Write to independent bookstore owners and don't forget the little man. Some little guys will stock your book before the big guys will. Write to your local hometown newspapers. Write to the grocery where your mom bought groceries when you were young and be sure to include how you remember going grocery shopping with your mother as a young child and how proud you would feel to see your book displayed on the shelves in your hometown. Who wouldn't be proud, after all? Don't forget to write to relatives you haven't seen in years. I did, and my aunt immediately sent a check to buy one of my books. Rack your brain and do some thinking, brainstorming. Then, make a list and start penning your way to marketability. Another tip, don't forget the powers of the Internet and take advantage of every free promotional opportunity you can find.

Barbara J. Robinson is the author of *Magnolia: A Wilting Flower* and *The Lord Had Something Better in Mind*

Rely on Faith

Dennis R. Ross

You know, as ironic as it may seem, I am not a trained writer. I'm a musician, and a spiritual Christian.

When, because of my search for security and the meaning of life, the spirit of God told me in 1975 — at the tender age of 18 — that I would write a book, I was both horrified and flabbergasted by the idea.

When family events brought about the inspiration and emotion to write *Dark Storm Coming*, it sealed the deal on the spiritual aspect of that guiding. When PublishAmerica accepted it, it made it a complete deal for me.

The following four years, as God directed me, I was able to get five books written, with four published by PublishAmerica. I just wrote from the seat of my pants, and used facts from the experiences in my heart. God did all the arranging, so I can thank God and PublishAmerica for my accomplishments.

Since I work in media advertising, I was able to be creative to make my own flyers and business cards, along with labels and posters regarding each of the books. I send them, at my own expense, to local Christian bookstores and churches. Since my work is entirely spiritual, I can target areas of greatest interest.

I will be submitting, to the faith columns of all my area newspapers, a self-written story of the books. There, truth will advertise the books for me, all I have to do is type it.

God said to go out and prosper in life. Truth will do that for you, if you have faith, and experience truth and inspiration for your own purpose. That way, your work will benefit the reader and yourself.

Advertising is easy; creativity makes it fun, so don't give up the moment something falls short.

It takes an average of three years for a self-made business to become prosperous. But in time, it will do its own work. Then you can be blessed with it. Good luck.

Dennis R. Ross is the author of *Dark Storm Coming,*
Trauma: Aiming for Beat One, Dark Core: A Transferrence of Trade,
Flesh and Blood: The Apostasy of Vanity

Surefire Success

Ron Shepherd

So the man walks up to this guy and says, "I wrote a book."

"Ya. Big deal. My cousin Louie did that once," and he walks away leaving you wondering what happened.

The opportunity to tell someone about your latest writing victory has just been shattered. The guy couldn't care less. You may not be a nobody, but you're close.

If you look back on the scene, the first thing you see is that the writer sure hasn't done his homework — totally unprepared and about as exciting as a boiled potato.

Now get back to the kitchen table and have a good talk with yourself. If you had been on the receiving end of this approach, the chances are pretty good that you'd have reacted the same way.

When you approached the guy, did you have any semblance of confidence or excitement in your voice? If you're not excited about the birth of your new book, how in William Webster's name can you expect the potential purchaser to be?

Where were you looking when you approached him? If you were checking out the mud on his Wellingtons, there was no air of confidence in your approach. Straighten up now and look him in the eye.

Pay attention now, Bippy. If you look like you've just been baptized in bad vinegar, that potential sale is about to go south on you before you even get to the starting line.

Everyone likes to be given something. Everyone. The problem is that they may just not be quite ready for the gift yet. If you're not a genius at the keyboard, go to a printing house and have them design a business card for you. On the left, put a picture of your book cover. Then put the name of your book in large letters, followed by where they can get the book.

Now comes the hard part. Do you walk up to a guy and say, "Ya want one of deese tings?" and shove one into his face? Gee willikers and doggone it anyway, NO. Your approach has to be business like and cannot enter their private space, that little spot of acreage we carry around with us.

Do you look like a person of authority? Dress the part. Look your best and you not only feel your best, but others will see you as a serious entity. You may like the feeling of the wind blowing through your hair, but let's face it, "You need a good haircut." Take all 24 of those earrings out and that bolt that runs through your nose. If you want to enter the world of high finance, you can't look like you shop at "Chez Goodwill." Gene Kelly in an old, very old, movie, sang a song that said "When there's a shine on your shoes, there's a melody in your heart." Believe me, he knew of what he speaketh.

"Cast not your pearls before swine." You might have heard that somewhere before. If the potential buyer is loading two tons of dirt with a shovel, go find another victim. If two people are in the middle of a conversation, please don't interrupt them. There has to be someone out there that would like to see your smiling face.

Let's go through an approach that has a chance for a successful outcome.

You see a nice young lady standing near the water cooler. She is looking over the daily paper. You walk up and take a drink of water from the cooler.

"How are you today?" Major eye contact.

"Today is a really big day for me. Today is the day my new book, *Clouds of Love*, is released. I am so darned excited."

"Are you an author?"

Well, duh! Of course you're an author. But just politely, in a self-effacing manner, say "Ayyuppp."

"Yes, I am. This is a really good book too."

Now. You have her attention. Your business card is primed and set to go off at any moment. You have the card already in your hand so that when you hand it to her, the front of the card is facing her so she can read it without fumbling. As she looks at it, give her a ten-word synopsis. No more than ten, darn it. You and she aren't best buddies, no matter how you wish it otherwise.

"I know you'd enjoy it. Have a nice day."

Now get lost and move on to the next potential buyer. With a thousand cards, you might just get some serious sales. Be honest and make good eye contact.

Well, these are just some of the basics of selling your new book. I'm sure you'll let your creative marketing genie out of the bottle and things will sell in a spectacular fashion. If the book is a slam-dunk winner, it could get wings and take off all on its own. The chances are pretty good, though, that your added help will take it a lot closer to the top, that itsy-bitsy small place where the good novels reside. Remember that if you're not excited about your book, don't expect anyone else to be.

Ron Shepherd is the author of *The River Calls* and *A River of Seasons*

A Few Quick Tips
Lou Sisk

These are some tips I found helpful.

1. My wife's hairdresser is planning to have a "Book Signing" night at her salon. She had a poster made up for the occasion. Seven or eight people have signed up for this event.

2. High school alumni printed material and annual "get togethers" are worth the effort.

3. There is a military-related website set up for the Army post where I was stationed in France. The purveyor of the website has given me a full page to help promote the book. He has had 37,000 hits since the beginning of the year 2000.

Lou Sisk is the author of *The Dark is All Gone*

Promotion is All About Courage
Pamela Skaggs

Now, didn't it take courage to sit down and write that masterpiece?

Weren't you led astray by every single distraction that could possibly destroy your focus from your vision? And time, was there ever enough time allowing you the opportunity to sit enmeshed in your manuscript? It took patience to focus your energies, and courage to create, follow through, and finally complete that dream.

Belief in yourself took heart. Trusting that, if you could control time, you would accomplish what few are able to do, and realize your possible future; knowing you would succeed, if given a chance, took courage. It was courage that helped you believe that one day your words would be appreciated by others. And it was that belief that motivated your desire to achieve this goal, putting it above and beyond other time constraints. You've wrestled with these obstacles. Your book is written and you've found a publisher who believes in you. Now the difficult part begins.

I decided early on to become active in local women's groups. Involvement in community service is an incredible opportunity to meet people. Most networking organizations offer time at each meeting to talk about your company and what you have to offer. I have found this a wonderful means to share my experiences, my work, and where individuals can purchase my novels. Don't be timid — take every opportunity to promote yourself. These people are there for the same reason you are.

In order to land a book signing, I used the old hard and fast approach — the telephone. I made a list from the Internet yellow pages and began my search for community relations' managers. After I obtained their name from the salesperson answering the phone, and found out the best time to call, I did so. Using my pitch, I asked if I could send them my press kit. That material includes my novel, a cover letter, my bio, the synopsis, as well as my press release, all neatly packaged in a folder with my business card attached. I make sure that the folder and the stationary are all color coordinated with the cover of my book. That first impression is very important. The books and supplies used for the kits are a tax write-off.

If the community relations' manager likes your pitch and wants to see your press kit, you have a good chance of scheduling that signing. I keep a spiral notebook with a date and time log where I document all the long-distance phone numbers for tax purposes. All documentation is important for future signings. I usually wait about two weeks after sending my press kit to call back and discuss the book signing. This method is simple, but I have had numerous book signings at some of the most prestigious areas in Southern California.

I have had book signings for both my novels at our local Barnes & Noble, and was told I could use them as a reference. Most of the larger corporations have district meetings with community relations' managers. Summon up the courage to ask your local bookseller if you can use their name to further your signings. The key to being assertive is honesty. Ask — all they can say is no.

I purchased a large banner with the title of my book and my name on it. At a signing, I attach this banner to my table. Many patrons are in such a hurry to get in and out of the bookstore they don't realize what you are there for, and this suggests a hint. I also bring See's candy to offer customers as they approach the area. This gives me the opportunity, while offering them candy, to start conversation, which opens the door. Some individuals may take up a great amount of your time wanting to know every detail of the writing and publishing process for their own benefit. I remain kind and generous with my time. I have found they usually decide to purchase, and will offer encouraging words for those approaching.

While speaking at writers' workshops, I have found the best-kept secret for relaxing and not being nervous, is to know your material. Go over it until you are absolutely sick of hearing yourself. When you understand your message thoroughly, this instills confidence. Share your journey into writing. Most potential authors are eager to learn about the process and interested in your story. I take the old-fashioned deep breaths before I go on, and this seriously helps to calm my nerves. They say nerves help motivate a speaker. You have accomplished much, so believe in yourself, know your material, take those deep breaths, and understand that to look fear in the face is to win that battle. Do that thing you fear to do, and the death of that fear is certain.

I usually ask those in attendance to fill out a name and address sheet for a drawing to be held following my presentation. After my discussion, I then raffle off prizes. By doing this, you will obtain all the names, addresses and e-mail addresses of those in attendance for future promotion of the new novel you are currently writing.

In closing, I would say believe in yourself enough to have the courage to get relatives, friends, business associates, your family doctor and dentist, as well as church and community affiliations informed. Nine times out of ten, they are so impressed that you have been published, they are excited about knowing you and thrilled to tell others. Don't be shy, have the courage and determination it took in the beginning to write your masterpiece, and know that others believe in you and what you have accomplished.

Pamela Skaggs is the author of *Ronnie, A Story of Triumph* and
Desires of the Heart, A Journey of Courage

It's All a Labor of Love
Julie Anne Swayze

Now that you have finally realized your dream and become a published author, the hard work begins. What is the best way to reach as many people as possible concerning your labor of love?

When I wrote my first novel, *Seth's Dominion*, all I wanted to do was get an agent, and have that agent find a publisher. When the book came out, I hadn't thought at all about marketing — this being quite odd since I have a degree in marketing. It would be wonderful if the book could sell itself, but just in case that doesn't happen, here are a few tips:

1. Build a website devoted to your book. List a brief biography, have a picture of the book cover, and a link to the PublishAmerica website. Plug any upcoming book-signing events that you will be participating in.

2. Contact all of your local chain and independent bookstores. I sent press kits. Include a brief bio, a synopsis of the book, the book, and any postcards or bookmarks of the cover. I inquired about any upcoming events that would feature local writers and new authors.

3. Use word of mouth. Even though I am naturally shy, I would talk up the book every chance I could — at work, the gym, family functions, bulletin boards.

I was happy with the results from my first book. However, with my second book, *O'Reilly's Ring*, coming out in a few months, I am adding something different to the items I described above. I plan on throwing a huge book-launch garden party this summer, but I am also hiring a publicist. Even though it is a huge expense, I'm hoping that it will generate additional sales.

Julie Anne Swayze is the author of *Seth's Dominion* and *O'Reilly's Ring*

You Make the Call!

Richard P. Tanos

In this, amidst the most rapid dynamic technological period of all time, please, do not forget, nor kid yourself, about the age-old profession, which most in the computer field refer to as being outdated, antiquated, and simply for a better word called...newspapers. Around the globe, there are still hundreds of thousands of what most Internet people call the dinosaur of information — newspaper companies. These newspaper companies, working still on a daily basis, constantly look for new, exciting, and interesting stories to write about. You, like me, as an author, really need to keep this in mind, since these newspaper companies are still valuable and provide a free, yes I did say free, resource that you and I can use in our efforts when it comes to marketing our books.

A previous ex-publisher, that I was affiliated with a few years ago, instructed me to attack hundreds of these newspapers by submitting a letter and a copy of my book asking, demanding, or even begging for a review. For a moment, put yourself in the same seat of that person working at that newspaper company, who is receiving daily the overwhelming multitude of book-review requests. Wow, kind of like being hit in the head with a board if you ask me. The results of this marketing tactic, which as far as I am concerned many publishers adhere to, can only remind me of one thing — junk mail. We all know what people do with junk mail; for those that don't, it is tossed it out.

We are getting closer to my point, now that you all understand the downside to what I lightly call, "Bombing Newspapers for Reviews." Instead of this wasteful, time-consuming, laborious exercise, I have found that if you take the time and locate your target newspaper company, make contact with the receptionist first and then hopefully the book reviewer second, your efforts will no doubt pay off. The physical newspaper locations you need to focus on are: possibly your childhood hometown, your current town, or perhaps a place where your novel is written about.

The Internet can provide all the contact information you will ever need. Get a phone number and take the time to make the call. Introduce yourself to the receptionist as an author and ask to speak with the on-staff book reviewer. They will always be courteous, perhaps asking questions about the book, and extremely helpful, and you will always be connected.

Once you get the person on the phone that you need to talk to, first explain that you would like to send them a copy of your book and second, for them to consider doing an article and possibly, but only if they like the novel, an interview. Obtaining a verbal authorization will guarantee that when your book arrives they will not toss it into the trash; besides, most of these book reviewers will agree with your request, especially when you are physically on the phone.

Timing on this kind of marketing is crucial. You need to have your book available for purchase since the article will direct potential customers to your own website or to the publisher's website. If you as an author do not have a website, you should strongly consider getting one — it is the future!

I have been told many times from either ex-publishers, agents, or marketing people, that as soon as the release date of your book is announced, it is sort of like acquiring a new car, where depreciation takes over forcing your car, and for that matter your novel, to become old news or possibly less valuable.

This may have been true many, many years ago, but in today's publishing environment, at least to me, this kind of thinking is nothing more than total hogwash. How can your book be outdated before it is available? Also, the customers you are trying to reach do not care one bit about when the book was released. As far as I am concerned, speaking from my own experience, the only date bookstore customers look at, but only if they are interested in that sort of thing, is usually the printing date, which is recorded on the first page of the book along with all the other boring stuff. Nevertheless, my point is that customers need something to trigger the sales switch in their heads, and to me, dates do not do this. Cutting to the chase of reality, if the topic of your novel interests the customer, they recognize your name, or perhaps the cover is stunning enough to attract above-average attention, they will certainly purchase.

In summary, spend a few timely telephone cents establishing a relationship with a contact person from within the newspaper location you are focusing on, and then, once you have established a confirmation with the resident book reviewer for the receipt of your novel, send your book along with a letter again confirming and thanking that person by name for the pending review and then offer your time for a possible interview. Your detail in personalizing your efforts will certainly pay off.

Richard P. Tanos is the author of *Pods*

Mindset Matters

David James Trapp

Perhaps the most realistic suggestion I ever read was that you, the author, must expect to do all of the promotion for the book. Anything the publisher does is an added bonus. It is up to you to get it done. Such a mindset is critical. It means you must give yourself an assignment every day to do something to promote the book. Send out a press release. E-mail someone. Post a flyer. Volunteer for a speech. Talk up your book with the clerk at the bookstore. Whatever. Do something. Be creative. Have a plan, then follow through with it. Only a handful of books effortlessly sell themselves. Yours isn't one of them. Don't give up your day job. Don't expect to get rich just because you've published a book. You wrote the book, perhaps as an expression of truth through the art of writing. That's good! Now keep going. You believe in your book, so go out and sell it. You're the best ambassador that your book has. And have fun. Never forget that promoting your book is part of the dream coming true.

Be blessed.

David James Trapp is the author of *Dog Days in Bedlam*

Be the Force: Four Easy Steps
Stephen Michael Verigood

Every book needs one thing: a force behind it to get it out to where the reading public can know about it. As the author, you are the force. Just as you created the idea behind the book, you can also create the demise of the book. It takes time for people to know about it, as there are thousands of books available. I used the following guidelines that I created for my first collection of my works, *My World's View: Poetry of a Deaf Child.*

— **Start locally.** Read your local newspaper to find out who handles the news for your particular area. If possible, send them an e-mail detailing that you are a local author with a book released, and in a very concise form, describe your book. Chances are, this person is going to forward the information to someone who may be interested in doing a story about you and your book.

— **Power of the Internet.** If you happen to know someone who does web media, or can create a webpage for you, inquire about seeing if they would help you create a page where people can find out more about you and your book. This is becoming a very powerful tool in today's world, and you would be very surprised at the amount of people who find out about you this way.

— **Contact groups/organizations geared towards your style.** Since my book is geared towards life as a deaf child, I have been in contact with deaf schools and other deaf organizations. If you wrote something about being a parent in today's society, you may want to contact groups/organizations that are geared towards helping parents. Again, you can find pretty much everything on the World Wide Web.

— **Most importantly, tell people about it.** My full-time job allows me to be in touch with a lot of people on a daily basis. I always try to have something with me that has my book title, my name, and my website on it. These people are most likely to go to their friends and tell them about it. Word of mouth is still the most powerful tool you can use, and it all starts with you. I have been on quite a few speaking engagements because all I did was tell someone that I was an author.

As an author, you may have the opportunity to do things that you would not ordinarily have the chance to do. Trying to do too much at one time can overwhelm you, so you have to pace yourself. Try to take care of one thing at a time. Before you know it, you may see the snowballing effects, and your book may be in for a long life.

Stephen Michael Verigood is the author of *My World's View: Poetry of a Deaf Child* and *To Chase a Heart: Volume One*

Creativity, Personality, and Persistence

Helen Vettori

The cliché, "It's not what you know, but whom you know," is true for those who have connections, but what about those of us who don't have those resources? Writing a book requires great effort alone. Getting that manuscript published is an extraordinary feat. But trying to market it becomes the most daunting challenge. Since your book is one of millions, the monumental problem of finding a way to make it stand out in a saturated marketplace may seem impossible. As with any challenge, however, success is quite possible by exploiting three characteristics: creativity, personality, and persistence.

Creativity really shouldn't be difficult for you. As a published author, you have proven not only to yourself, but to a publisher that inspiration has allowed you to craft a book that will interest others. It doesn't matter whether your book is fiction or non-fiction. All forms of writing require skill and creativity to develop something that people want to read.

Employ the same passion you devoted to writing when devising efforts for marketing. Think not only of obvious venues to contact, but unusual ones, too. The corporate-directed, mega bookstores rarely encourage unknown authors. Small, family-owned bookstores may welcome you, but your strategy to approach the owners must make you appear extraordinary, and, therefore, intriguing. Likewise, coffee shops, PTAs, fairs, senior centers or assisted-living homes, specialty shops like museum stores, community service or social groups and book clubs will want you to appear if you successfully sell yourself.

Your book may become a bestseller, but before that recognition, *you* are the *hook*. A public relations executive gave me the following valuable insight. People are primarily interested in people. In other words, outline what makes you unique, and then emphasize that.

Confidence and professionalism are key. You have only seconds to grab the attention of whomever you're contacting. Whenever possible, meet in person. Dress appropriately. First impressions will dictate how well someone will receive you. Smile, shake hands as you introduce yourself, and make a pleasant greeting. Then, hand the person your card. You can easily make a business card on the computer, or you can have a print shop create one for you. Putting the cover of your book on the card is effective because the picture will imprint much more readily than the other necessary information. Next, quickly yet eloquently explain that you are an author seeking to appear at their location. Then, give a brief synopsis of your book in no more than fifteen seconds without stumbling over your words. You must practice, practice, practice before you go out. You may even consider attending a public speaking or acting class. In addition to your business card, prepare an 8 ½ x11 promotional handout to leave. At some point in the conversation, ask for his or her business card, and shake hands as you say goodbye. Finally, make a follow-up call a day or two later, and try to schedule a firm date for you to appear.

If you're unsuccessful in making a firm date for an appearance, jot down a note to yourself to call again in a reasonable amount of time. Persistence may be the only way to close a deal. Unfortunately, there is a fine line between persistence and harassment. Be aware of subliminal or even blatant negative messages.

My favorite negative response came from a bookstore manager. He told me his store had scheduled authors all summer, and thereafter he'd be interested only in "fall" books. Just what is a "fall" book? Nothing. That was his way of telling me he wasn't interested in what I had to offer. If something similar happens to you, don't get discouraged. Just because one option is dead, there can be many more opportunities. You must approach seldom-tapped establishments. You may hear, "No," but you'll never find those "Yes" answers without asking.

When a letter is more appropriate to send than for you to meet someone personally, keep your *hook* concise. Call the business to get the name of someone likely to be interested in your "pitch," and send it addressed to that person. Send only one 8 ½ x11 page unless you wish to include a press release. You may wish to staple your business card to the letter, or you may wish to have letterhead that imparts the information necessary for someone to respond to you. Making an attractive yet simple letterhead is effortless on a computer. Be careful not to make a design that requires more than a glance to glean information. Send the letter Confirmation Delivery, and track it to ensure it was received. Call the individual you sent the letter to a day or two after she or he received the letter to follow-up personally. Once again, listen for cues that will tell you whether or not this person is interested. If you sense anything positive, try to pin down a date at that time, or follow-up with a second call.

Once you have an invitation to speak, make it work for you. Create a presentation that will showcase you and your book. Weave your personal experiences into the lecture. I recommend a Power Point production or slide show. Audiences prefer speeches with graphics. Most organizations and individuals are delighted to provide images for recognition in return. Additionally, it's imperative that you notify the media. That way the media can inform the public about your coming event, and may be enticed to assign reporters to cover you and your book.

In our fast-paced society, those who make the decisions to promote authors find it easy to disregard impersonal marketing queries. Imparting a charismatic aura will make a difference. If you are unforgettable to that person, he or she is much more likely to invite you and to promote you and your book. Therefore, be creative, be personable, and be persistent. Once you have small marketing successes, larger ones should follow.

Helen Vettori is the author of *Missions of Our Moment*

Marketing Bliss for Published Authors

Joe Vojt

Promoting yourself is a one-way experience and can't be measured instantly. You are forced to be constantly creative. Always look and think of new ideas that might spark interest in your work. Because name recognition is the hardest factor to overcome, you need to keep your creative juices flowing.

The first rule that will help in the marketing maze is the basic question, "What makes your novel stand out?" You, the published author, need to identify that scope of interest. Once you have identified your target area, then you need to apply the resources available before moving onto the next challenge. Again you, the published author, are best qualified to come up with ideas on how to transform your hard work into interesting forms of mass-media tools. The Internet is a great resource, but local and national coverage still requires that old-type snail mail. You need to step beyond the newspapers, libraries, radio station, bookstores, etc. in order to target areas of your choosing. Here, the need is to utilize the blanket coverage concept.

Examples: One is an effective press release, limited to one page, and covering your specific novel target. Utilize a brief synopsis, or even a section of your work that will attract the attention you expect. Just like the hook in the first few pages of your novel, you have to pare it down to only a hundred words. If the novel has been reviewed, place that information so it stands out. The object is to generate interest in your creative accomplishment.

Another item is a colored bookmark. Here you create with your target area in mind. Use a colorful business card with a brief but eye-catching script from your work. The bookmark and business card should have a limited number of items on them (i.e. novel cover, ISBN number, website, and e-mail with those carefully selected words highlighted from your novel). This is like placing words on a dime. Make it worthwhile. All these items can be produced on the computer with a color printer and quality photo-grade paper. The cost is reasonable for the quantity you need when doing mass mailing. A paper cutter would allow you to produce both volume and consistent copies. As my goal, I would snail mail ten items every week to what I considered high-profile mailings.

I can give you an illustration of how that worked. My aim was manufacturing quality and the target I used was mailing the top 100 CEOs in my state with two bookmarks. Another area I used was manufacturing consulting and service organization in my six state regions. Again, all this promotion is one way. You can't tell how well you have done until you receive your royalties.

Another interesting idea I employed was to place one of my business cards into every bill or correspondence I mailed out. I also created miniature color labels of the book cover that I place on the outside of every envelope being mailed. This is the type of commitment that is required to market your work.

The bliss in all this is simple. You never give up and continue regardless of the results. Once your name becomes known and accepted, you have the potential to begin increasing your sales. Good luck, and keep on being creative. Feel proud of the accomplishments you have made.

Joe Vojt is the author of *Threshold of Consciousness* and
Threshold of Consciousness II

Retain Your Goals

Helene Vorce-Tish

Without promotion, the book virtually remains hidden from view. The motives for writing a book would logically include: money, recognition, and the desire to have the story or ideas reach out and "speak" to as many people as possible. The goals for writing would therefore be the goals for promotion.

Once the book has been published, it is important for the author to consider ways to promote the book. Some ways can be very expensive; others are very simple. Yet, all methods should be considered.

This is the direction I took: I pursued television, local public-access TV, and radio opportunities. I have been interviewed on local public-access TV four times. I was successful participating in an authors' panel at a Barnes & Noble bookstore. Our group did a great deal of promotion for this event, such as calling friends and people who might be interested, and being interviewed on the radio by a well-known radio personality. Try bookstore signings. Remember to put up posters in the shopping area and place press releases in newspapers.

Local clubs and organizations are an excellent source for promotion. Check the local newspaper and small presses for club calendars. Call these clubs and organizations for speaking opportunities. These organizations vary in interests. Books contain themes, so the topics can be slanted toward the members' interests. Consider all organizations besides writers' groups. Try to get directories of local and state-wide organizations. Consider contacting senior residences and care facilities. Booklets are available for different localities.

Get to the meeting a little early so that you can get acquainted with some of the members. Try to introduce a little humor into your talk. Smile. Let people know that you are having some fun, and, in doing so, you are reaching out and establishing some rapport. Include them with your ideas and comments. Try to build up suspense in your talk, so that people will want to read your story — don't spend too much time talking about your book, so decide when to stop and tell them that you will sign books for them.

When making contacts with activities' directors or program chairmen, offer to fax them information about your book, your bio, and credits, as well as your website address.

Join local writers' groups for personal contacts and ideas. Look for speaking opportunities at conventions and workshops. Consider doing your own workshops with local recreation groups.

Your own personal webpage is also very important. It can contain color photos of your books and of yourself. Here, a person can browse the information about your books and interesting information about yourself.

Look for opportunities to have your book reviewed in area newspapers.

Contact bookstores and groups beyond your own locality.

Talk to other authors, attend seminars on promotion, and persevere. After all, it is your book, your ideas, and a part of you is on every page; so reach out, explore, and create. The world is waiting and listening.

Helene Vorce-Tish is the author of *The Wounds of Hate* and
Challenging the Forces of Hate

Ways to Promote Your Book
Ruth Weidig

The Internet: There are many free websites. If you can't design your own page, sample pages to copy are available without charge. Also, get free advertising on the webpages that show your short ad. In return for the privilege, you will see spot ads across the top of your webpage.

E-mail:Every message you send should have mention of your book(s), latest release, publisher and webpage. Example:
Now on sale: (Insert title of your book here)
Publisher's address
I invite you to visit my webpage: (Insert your website link here)

Chat Room: Join literary/writers' chat rooms and introduce yourself as an author. Visit often to keep your name and that of your publisher up front.

Brochures & Bookmarks: Make your own brochures and bookmarks. Inexpensive and fun. Great for sneaking into bill payments, doctor offices, hotel lobbies, just about anywhere people congregate. Each time your latest book is released, stuff those envelopes. Don't forget to mail one to your friends and business associates.

Speaking Engagements: A great personal contact. It gives the audience the opportunity to know you. At the same time, it affords you the opportunity to promote your work, and is usually an invitation to sell your books. And it's fun.

News Media: A press release with the author's picture, a brief synopsis of the book, writing credits, and reviews packaged in a commercial folder can be a helpful tool in capturing an editor's interest. Don't forget to include your business card. If you are lucky enough to have a newspaper interested, invite the editor to your home for a friendly chat. Editors are very inquisitive about the author and will often ask to take the author's photograph for the article.

In conclusion: Books do not sell themselves. Authors must be their own promotional representatives.

Ruth Weidig is the author of *The Color of Love*

How I Intend to Promote My Novel

David A. Wilson

I have been on Cloud 9 since learning that PublishAmerica was going to publish my Civil War/vampire novel, *Curse of the Vampire*.

Now that it is getting very close to the time that it will be out in print, I have much work to do in promoting it, and I will have to do that at the same time that I get ready to produce yet another Halloween vampire comedy play that I have written, *Barbara Nolan Meets the Mummy*. It will be lots of work, but I can handle it, and just love the challenge.

I have been at work for some time in promoting my book. I have made arrangements with the lady at the local bookstore for her to get in copies of my book and to have me there for a signing. One of the associate editors of the local newspaper has promised me that he is really going to give me a big write-up when *Curse of the Vampire* comes out.

I have found a most economical way of promoting my book. I have taken a news release about my book being published, that appeared in a local paper, and made photocopies for only six cents per copy.

When I talk to local people about my novel, I give them one of these copies, which reads: "Grantville Native Publishes Civil War Vampire Novel." When I meet someone who lives outside of my area or even in another state, I give those people one of the copies that includes information on how someone can get a copy of my book, should it not be in stock at their local bookstore.

I am really beginning to use these along with copies of how my book cover will look. The latter I give to bookstore owners, and I gave one to the lady who stocks books at the local supermarket where I buy my groceries.

I am really talking this book up. I addressed a summer recreation group in

Grantville about it, with a good response from the kids and adults in the audience.

I am also planning on printing business cards which will have my name, phone number, title of the book, e-mail address, and my website (*www.david-a-wilson.com*).

I really know a lot of people from my eight years as a grocery bagger at a supermarket, my three years as a city councilman in Grantville, Georgia, my being active in church work, and being a local playwright — having put on three vampire comedy plays on the weekend before Halloween to raise money toward restoring the old auditorium where these plays are performed.

We are going to do another play in this series that I wrote, *Barbara Nolan Meets the Mummy*, and I am donating a copy of *Curse of the Vampire* as a door prize to be drawn after the play. My plays draw a lot of people and media attention, and I believe *Mummy* and *Curse* will help one another. My strategy for promoting the book is to do great locally, and try to get my book well known all over Georgia. There's a good chance that I'm going to be on a radio show, heard all over the South, where I call in regularly.

Overall, I am going to give it all that I have and I just hope that my book will do well. I love to write and would love to make my living at it.

David A. Wilson is the author of *Curse of the Vampire*

Promoting a Published Author
Katha Winther

My background includes:

— marketing department (seven years) at a large company, observing phenomenal sales representatives in action

— music editor (eight years) at a large publishing company. Additional responsibilities included contacting record-label companies, convincing (begging) them to send newly released compact discs to our company for inclusion in our publication

— TV host on America's Shopping Channel — on-air "live" five hours a day/five days a week, selling merchandise in a fast-paced environment

— singing national anthems for several professional teams, beating out the competition when they already had hundreds of demo tapes on hand

My personality and background naturally lend themselves to marketing. My father was involved in politics for many years — I was able to observe a "pro schmoozer" in action.

Marketing skills can be applied to many different areas — marketing is marketing, whatever the product may be.

My tips:

Psyche yourself up, and get some internal enthusiasm about your book. Talk it up wherever you go. Be persistent, but not obnoxious. Always have a supply of business cards with you to hand out. Word of mouth is great! I handed out several cards after my yoga class recently because someone had overheard me talking about my book.

Use your book's cover art to make promotional materials. I've made business cards, flyers, bookmarks, brochures, envelopes, and stickers. Regularly stick one of your promotional items in every envelope you mail out — even bills. Put a note on it "Please buy my book!"

Buy some good card stock paper at your local copy center — about ten cents per sheet. I can get three bookmarks on a page. A great website to visit for bookmarks, using Microsoft Word, is: *www.personal-computer-tutor.com/paperbookmarks.htm.*

Use your website effectively. Put all necessary ordering information on the page, and make it sound like a quick and easy process. Encourage your friends and family to e-mail information about your book to their friends. Give some reasons for ordering your book, and encourage them to order more than one. They can keep one for themselves, and save one for gift-giving time also, because they're nice people and doing a favor for a friend. You get my drift — whatever works.

Add a blurb about your book to any weekly/monthly bulletin (printed or online) to any club/organization/church that you may be affiliated with. Contact your local newspaper or hometown paper — try to get something put in print about your book. Columnists are always looking for hooks/angles/slants; try to have something unique to tell them about yourself.

Don't let anyone discourage you! I recently called a bookstore in an upscale neighborhood and spoke with the woman in charge of book signings. She talked about the events in rather disparaging words: (1) the signings take place at night, no other stores are open, there isn't much "foot traffic," people are on their way to restaurants; (2) the author in many cases provides them with a list of 200 people to invite, and only 20 people will show up; (3) even if you have written *Gone With the Wind* (or equivalent), it's a tough market, and your book won't go anywhere unless you "push it"; (4) you need to get yourself prepared for rejection, etc.

I told her that I was used to rejection sometimes, but that it didn't stop me at all — I'm persistent! She said that I had already won a quarter of the battle. A "can-do" positive attitude works well when trying to get your foot in the door at bookstores. The bottom line for bookstores is making money by selling books. They want to know what's in it for them. I told her that if my book was in their store, it would just "fly off the shelves." Of course, I believe in myself and my book.

Keep a list of who you've contacted and when. I made a book-contact database using Microsoft Works. If you've talked to anyone, always thank them for their time. Follow up with a cover letter, brochure, etc. and put it in the mail promptly. If you plan to call the bookstore or company in the future, write down a reminder somewhere. I use Microsoft Outlook's calendar feature as a pop-up reminder.

Drug stores and supermarkets have book sections, too. Ask the manager